JUVENILE JUSTICE
in AMERICA

Kennikat Press
National University Publications
Multi-disciplinary Studies in the Law

General Editor
Rudolph J. Gerber
Arizona State University

JUVENILE JUSTICE
in AMERICA

VICTOR L. STREIB

National University Publications
KENNIKAT PRESS // 1978
Port Washington, N. Y. // London

Manufactured in the United States of America

Published by
Kennikat Press Corp.
Port Washington, N.Y./London

Library of Congress Cataloging in Publication Data

Streib, Victor L
    Juvenile Justice in America.

    (Multi-disciplinary studies in the law) (National University publications)
    Bibliography: p.
    Includes index.
    1. Juvenile justice, Administration of—United States. 2. Juvenile delinquency—United States. 3. Juvenile delinquency—United States—Prevention. I. Title.
HV9104.S843   364'.973   78-5309
ISBN 0-8046-9212-2

CONTENTS

FIGURES

PREFACE

As with many researcher-teacher-practitioners, I migrated to juvenile justice only after a first interest in criminal justice. My interest began with a concern for crime and even more concern for society's curious reaction to crime. Analysis of the harshness of criminal justice led me to examine the juvenile justice system as a fascinating experiment in socialized justice. Replacing punishment with treatment and "focus on the act" with "focus on the person" are quite seductive concepts.

Several years of research, teaching, and practice in juvenile justice have revealed for me some of the truths behind the rhetoric and good intentions. Each time Justice Fortas speaks to us from *Kent* and *Gault,* I understand further the brilliant clarity of his message. It may take many more years before I can contribute—if I ever can—meaningful answers to the important questions. This is my beginning.

This book is based upon current and historic law, published literature, interviews with juvenile justice professionals, conversations with delinquent children, oral questions and written term papers from my students, and personal experience as attorney and prosecutor for too many delinquent children. As a researcher I have studied a wide range of juvenile justice statutes and cases, both past and current. I have studied the literature from scholars, practitioners, and observers. I have talked at length with anyone who knew anything about juvenile justice, the best sources being the recipients of juvenile justice services. As an attorney specializing in juvenile justice, I have lived the participant-observer's dream. I have been a working functionary within juvenile justice systems from before apprehension to after parole revocation. I have had opportunity to advise and counsel prosecutors, judges, probation officers, institutional personnel, and informal youth counselors. I did not simply observe as a professor doing research; I actually became a part of the system I was studying.

Like all researchers, I owe much to many persons. For the time, facilities, and university support, I am indebted to Dr. J. Erroll Miller and Indiana University. For priceless intellectual stimulation and encouragement I single out Dr. David R. Walters of Indiana University. That most compelling factor—the need to do something about juvenile justice—was provided by the many juvenile justice children I came to know, most memorably Jackie, Linda, Angela, Mark, Gordon, Billy, and Gerry. I have concluded that these children can point to important solutions if we can turn off our rhetoric long enough to hear them.

JUVENILE JUSTICE
in AMERICA

ABOUT THE AUTHOR

Victor L. Streib is associate professor of Forensic Studies at Indiana University, Bloomington. He is also an attorney specializing in juvenile cases. Prior professional activities included periods as a juvenile court prosecutor and as a research scientist in socio-legal systems research. He has written various articles on facets of American law.

1. INTRODUCTION

The Juvenile Justice System (JJS) as it typically functions in America's thousands of jurisdictions in the late 1970s is our subject. For our purposes the JJS is defined as that sociolegal process having responsibility and authority for public reaction to current juvenile delinquency and deterrence of future juvenile delinquency, including within that process the public and private agents, agencies, laws, rules, and policies having to do with juvenile delinquency. By "sociolegal process" is meant a particular method of performing tasks and accomplishing goals which is based upon and governed by public law and which operates within and is affected by a company of interdependent individuals. The concept of "juvenile delinquency" includes acts defined by law as acts of delinquency, including violations of criminal laws or ordinances, as well as status offenses such as habitual truancy, incorrigibility, immoral conduct, and curfew violations (Fox, 1972: 226-27). The public and private agencies involved include police, court, and correctional agencies as well as youth service bureaus, mental health clinics, drug abuse counselors, and school counselors. We will exclude the processing of dependent or neglected children, which is an important sociolegal process but beyond the scope of this work.

The purpose of this work is to complement the many good works on juvenile law (Fox, 1972; Miller et al., 1971; Ketcham and Paulsen, 1967; and others) which present quite sophisticated analyses of the legal issues but sometimes insufficiently address the functional JJS process and the nonlegal problems and issues which arise during this process. If we accomplish our objectives, we will reveal in detail the functioning of the JJS in the real world and the often glaring gaps between juvenile justice academic theory and juvenile justice system practice. Most importantly, we will probe the reasons that these gaps exist and suggest some means for closing them.

This analysis is purposely rather narrow and unique. It views the JJS as primarily in part a production line whose purpose is to process selected children from beginning to end in the most efficient manner possible. Of course, efficiency does not guarantee effectiveness, but neither should efficiency make effectiveness harder to achieve. A major purpose herein is to reveal those points within the JJS at which effectiveness and efficiency clash and the manner in which that clash has been and can be resolved.

This is an analysis of the entire JJS as a system. Each particular function, agent, agency, decision, or policy is examined in the context of the overall system operation and systemic goals and objectives. Clashes between systemic goals and policies and agent/agency goals and policies will be particularly illustrated. Moreover, pervading the entire analysis must be concern for the two masters of the JJS: the best interests of the child and the best interests of society. Serving two masters is always difficult and at times impossible, so the JJS is probably incapable of success in any absolute meaning of that term. However, during each microanalysis of a JJS function the system's goals as well as its masters must also be considered.

The primary focus is the JJS of the late 1970s. However, as with all sociolegal systems, a meaningful current analysis must be preceded by a basic understanding of the history and fundamental characteristics of the system. Chapter 2 presents this basic information in a cursory manner, including the historical development of the JJS, the legal system/ social system characteristics of the JJS, and JJS goals and operating principles.

The first of two primary divisions is the functional description and analysis of the JJS presented in chapter 3. This information is presented through flow charts and discourse. After digesting this detailed analysis the reader should turn to the problems and recommendations which are the second primary division. These problems and recommendations are divided into sections of philosophy and design (chapter 4), operations (chapter 5), effects (chapter 6), and the informal JJS (chapter 7). These problems and recommendations are purposely written in an argumentative manner to provoke interest and in-depth consideration. Chapter 8 presents the conclusions.

2. HISTORY AND CHARACTERISTICS OF THE JJS

ORIGIN OF THE JJS

Because the first formal juvenile court was so labeled on July 1, 1899 (Illinois Juvenile Court Act of 1899), it is too often assumed that the JJS is therefore little more than three-quarters of a century old. However, the origins of the various components of the JJS go back much further than that (Sanders, 1970; Cogan, 1970). The notion of separate treatment for children under criminal law goes back to a very early English law. Children under seven years of age were legally incapable of committing a crime, and children between seven and fourteen were presumed incapable, this concept being based upon a child's inability to have a guilty mind, or *mens rea.* Thus, from almost the beginning of Anglo-American law children have been treated differently from adults who commit the same acts (Rendleman, 1971).

Even for those children convicted of crimes under early criminal law, the actual punishment was less severe. And even after convictions for capital offenses death sentences were often not carried out for children (Sanders, 1945). In other cases the jury would refuse to convict if a child were facing the death penalty for a comparatively minor offense. The king's pardoning power was used often to save children from execution. Thus, not only did the law make children a special class of criminal but in the functioning of the criminal justice system children were treated somewhat more "gently" than adults (Dyson and Dyson, 1968).

The origin of juvenile corrections in the United States goes back at least to the opening of the New York House of Refuge in 1825 (Fox, 1970). This house of refuge was established to meet the same kinds of needs the JJS of the 1970s tries to meet, including avoidance of harsh criminal penalties for unfortunate children, segregating "predelinquent" children from hardened delinquents, providing "proper" moral, ethical, political, and social values and role models for deprived children, and treating such children as victims rather than offenders.

Another example is the Chicago Reform School established in 1855 to serve, not punish, the same class of crime-prone children (Fox, 1970). Such a reform school was seen as a necessary alternative to placing children in adult institutions. In fact, the reform movement in Illinois leading to the 1899 establishment of the first official juvenile court was characterized partly by a desire to avoid prisons for children by establishing a special juvenile court which could not send children to prison (Fox, 1970).

The social and political roots of the juvenile court are not altogether clear. Traditionally it was thought that the nineteenth-century reform movement concerned with the welfare of children gave birth to a scientific, objective, and dispassionate juvenile court which would reform and develop wayward children (Besharov, 1974; Mennel, 1972). Alternatively, it has been persuasively argued that the advent of the juvenile court heralded a retrenchment in correctional practice, a regression in poor-law policy, and an encouragement to reach into children's private lives with punitive policies disguised in the rhetoric of rehabilitation (Fox, 1970; Platt, 1969). In any event, there is reason to believe that early criminal courts traditionally took a somewhat fatherly and protective attitude toward children, whether to offer humanitarian assistance or parental punishment. This special attitude toward children was written into law and required of juvenile courts (Schultz, 1973).

The notion of a special juvenile court caught on quickly, and other states began to follow Illinois's example. By 1912 almost half the states had juvenile court legislation; by 1925 all states but two had such legislation, with the federal government passing a juvenile court act in 1938 (Ruppert, 1971-72). Thus, by 1925 it is fair to conclude that the JJS existed in all critical elements, in law if not in fact. Jurisdictions were somewhat less expeditious in implementing JJS legislation than they were in passing it (Johnson, 1975: 5).

In sum, the concept of special treatment of children under law is several hundred years old, the concept of a separate juvenile court is 75 years old, the concept of special institutions for children is at least 150 years old, and the concept of a somewhat cohesive *system* of juvenile justice is at least 50 years old. This system of juvenile justice, along with its various components and subsystems, has been a part of American jurisprudence for enough time for us to understand it and evaluate it.

It is not "old" by comparison with other American legal systems, such as the criminal justice system or the mental health disposition system, but it has had its chance to perform and demonstrate whatever value it may have to our society.

SOCIALIZED ERA OF THE JJS

From the beginning of the JJS (arbitrarily established as 1899) until the United States Supreme Court decision in *In re Gault* in 1967, the JJS operated under a concept of law and justice "... so altered as to be virtually unrecognizable in any traditional sense" (Faust and Brantingham, 1974: 145). Rather than a legal system which reacts to violations of law or which provides a forum for resolution of legal disputes, the socialized JJS attempted to intervene *before* serious violations of law occurred. The socialized JJS tried to predict future behavior of the individual involved, rather than deliberating over evidence as to past criminal acts of the individual involved. Rather than provide typical governmental services to a citizen, the socialized JJS was to offer approximately the same care, custody, and discipline that a loving parent would offer to a child.

The socialized JJS is often presented as an adaptation of the medical model as it might be applied to troubled children: "early identification, diagnosis, prescription of treatment, implementation of therapy, and cure or rehabilitation under aftercare supervision" (Faust and Brantingham, 1974: 147). The rhetoric from this era is striking for its presumptuousness:

The judges of the juvenile court, in exercising jurisdiction, have, in accordance with the most advanced philanthropic thought, recognized that the lack of proper home care can best be supplied by the true foster parent (the state). (Mack, 1909: 105)

The action is not for the trial of a child charged with a crime, but is mercifully to save it from such an ordeal, with the prison or penitentiary in its wake, if the child's own good and the best interests of the state justify such salvation. Whether the child deserves to be saved by the state is no more a question for a jury than whether the father, if able to save it, ought to save it. (*Commonwealth v. Fisher,* 1905)

Beginning in 1899 with separate legislation, separate court hearings, probation supervision, and institutional segregation, the socialized JJS set about achieving the lofty goals established for it. That it never achieved any of these goals is now generally accepted (*Kent v. United States; In re Gault*). However, during the almost seventy years of its existence it progressively pursued those goals.

The socialized JJS embraced five pivotal philosophical elements:
1. The superior rights of the state over the rights of the child and his parents;
2. Individualized justice for each child;
3. The juvenile status of delinquency as somewhat different from and less serious than the adult status of criminal;
4. Informal, noncriminal procedure instead of legalistic, criminal procedure; and
5. A remedial, preventive, correctional purpose rather than a punitive, threatening purpose. (Caldwell, 1966: 362-63)

A key element separating the socialized JJS from the constitutionalized JJS is informal, noncriminal procedure. This element is not difficult to appreciate if considered in context with the overall goals of the JJS. Consider other child-serving agencies today for comparison. Is it not typical in agencies whose purpose is to help needy children to want to do so with as little resistance from outsiders as possible? Do charitable organizations expect the recipients of their free goods and services to challenge these gifts and to exercise extensive rights to refuse these gifts?

Consider the JJS as the supreme foster parent. Acting in the capacity of parent, the state might well expect almost absolute obedience to its parental admonitions, much as natural parents expect their child to wear his boots on a rainy day or to stay in bed with a bad cold. The concept of the child having extensive rights to effectively challenge such parental guidance and care is foreign to our society. Parents have, within very wide guidelines, total, unchallengeable authority to force the child to do "what is best for him." Thus, if a special system was being established to act in behalf of the parent, it is not surprising that a similar total, unchallengeable authority was given to that special system.

Aside from the government-as-parent role, private citizens have traditionally had more difficulty in preventing beneficial services from the government than in preventing nonbeneficial services. Moreover, such preventive activity seems to be most uncommon. How often do citizens exercise legal maneuvers to avoid receipt of a tax refund, repaving of their street, or more police protection for their neighborhood? Similarly, the designers of the JJS might understandably have assumed that private citizens, here juveniles and their parents, would have little desire or need for mechanisms for avoiding the beneficial services offered to them by the JJS.

The socialized JJS was functionally much like the present constitutionalized JJS, except for the legal steps and functions required by *In re Gault* and its progeny. A child was commonly brought to court by a police officer or another responsible adult, such as a school counselor, neighbor, or parent. The judge would consider the case in an informal conference and examine the allegations against the child and any evidence for the child. On the basis of this conference the judge would decide upon the child's delinquent status. If delinquency was found, the judge would order an appropriate disposition, which could be probation, institutionalization, or some other "treatment" mode. Thus, all the basic functions were performed in the socialized JJS that are performed in the constitutionalized JJS, albeit in a much more informal and perfunctory manner. The socialized JJS simply left presentation of the child's side of the case to the same system agent responsible for presentation of the state's side of the case. It is misleading to characterize the socialized JJS as disregarding or denying the child's side of the story.

To return to the medical model and parent/child analogy, the juvenile respondent was seen as a sick infant, and the socialized JJS was the Solomon-wise parent/physician/child psychologist. The socialized JJS did not permit the juvenile respondent to deny the delinquency manifested by the misbehavior, just as the physician doesn't permit the sick infant to deny the disease indicated by the fever, coughing, and other physiological symptoms. The socialized JJS, like the physician, simply observed the child very closely, diagnosed the problem, and ordered an expeditious cure. To give children, with all their inherent immaturity and lack of knowledge, a concrete opportunity to prevent some of these symptoms from being examined or to prevent implementation of the cure would have been improper behavior for a parent or a physician, or for a state acting as a parent or physician.

The socialized JJS split from the comparatively legalistic criminal justice system (CJS) in 1899 and spent perhaps the first thirty or forty years of its sixty-eight-year life trying to match its rhetoric with action. It progressively became more and more "socialized" in that it tried more new and individualized treatment techniques to react to delinquency. The constitutionalized JJS which replaced it in 1967 was also more rhetoric than action during the first few years of its life (Lefstein et al., 1969); it has only recently become what could be called truly legalistic, or constitutionalized.

CONSTITUTIONALIZED ERA OF THE JJS

The term "constitutionalized" should not mislead one into assuming that the socialized JJS did not operate under the provisions of the United States Constitution and the various state constitutions. The JJS has always been a system of law and as such has always been governed generally by constitutions. However, the Warren Court found many applications of constitutional privileges and rights in the criminal justice area during the 1960s and subsequently transplanted most of the newly found constitutional rights of adult criminal defendants into the JJS for the assumed benefit of juvenile delinquent respondents. The beginning of the constitutionalized era of the JJS is set as 1967, the year the United States Supreme Court decided *In re Gault*. This is the point after which juvenile courts were required to follow certain constitutional guidelines, even though several juvenile courts were following similar legalistic guidelines before 1967 and even more juvenile courts were following the socialized, informal guidelines after 1967. Thus, the terminal points of the constitutionalized JJS are no more clear-cut than the terminal points of the socialized JJS. Nevertheless, there are two, rather distinct eras of the JJS for analytical purposes.

The constitutionalization of the JJS was anticipated in 1966 by *Kent v. United States:*

While there can be no doubt of the original laudable purpose of juvenile courts, studies and critiques in recent years raise serious questions as to whether actual performance measures well enough against theoretical purpose to make tolerable the immunity of the process from the reach of constitutional guaranties applicable to adults. . . . There is evidence, in fact, that there may be grounds for concern that the child receives the worst of both worlds: that he gets neither the protections accorded to adults nor the solicitous care and regenerative treatment postulated for children. (*Kent*, at 555-56)

Earlier cases had indicated that the Fourteenth Amendment and incorporated constitutional rights apply to children as well as to adults (*Haley v. State of Ohio* [1948] and *Gallegos v. State of Colorado* [1962]).

While *Kent* had held that the waiver hearing must respect the essentials of constitutional due process and fair treatment, *Gault* held that such is also the case for adjudicatory hearings as a requirement of the due process clause of the Fourteenth Amendment to the U. S. Constitution. For the particular facts of *Gault*, Fourteenth Amendment due process included proper notice of the charges and hearings to the child and his parents, right to effective counsel for the delinquent respondent at the adjudicatory hearing, right to confront and cross-examine adverse witnesses, and right not to be a witness against one's self.

Within a few years after *Gault* the United States Supreme Court had decided two other major cases dealing with the Fourteenth Amendment and the JJS. In *In re Winship* (1970) the Court held that proof beyond a reasonable doubt is among the essentials of due process and fair treatment required by *Gault* during the adjudicatory stage. The Court's opinion was limited to cases in which the juvenile is charged with an act which would constitute a crime if committed by an adult. The primary bases for this holding were the firm place of the reasonable doubt standard within Fourteenth Amendment due process, the comparable seriousness of a felony prosecution and a finding of delinquency resulting in loss of liberty for several years, and a belief that the reasonable doubt standard would not destroy the beneficial aspects of the juvenile process.

The *Winship* majority opinion had reaffirmed, just three years after *Gault*, the requirements of Fourteenth Amendment due process as they affect the adjudicatory hearing within the JJS. However, the majority opinion was written by Mr. Justice Brennan during the waning days of the so-called liberal Warren Court. A harbinger of things to come might well be Mr. Chief Justice Burger's persuasive dissent:

... I dissent from further strait-jacketing of an already overly-restricted system. What the juvenile court systems need is not more but less of the trappings of legal procedure and judicial formalism; the juvenile system requires breathing room and flexibility in order to survive, if it can survive the repeated assaults from this Court. (*Winship*, at 376)

But one year later the United States Supreme Court issued a JJS majority opinion in which Mr. Chief Justice Burger could join. In *McKeiver v. Pennsylvania* (1971) the Court considered the last of the trappings of Fourteenth Amendment due process: right to trial by jury. However, instead of taking this final step in the application of the generally accepted accouterments of due process, the Court held that trial by jury in the JJS adjudicatory hearing is not a constitutional requirement. Taking exhaustive measures to justify this holding, Mr. Justice Blackmun's plurality opinion argued that the Court had regularly refrained from imposing all criminal procedure rights upon the JJS, that influential advisory agencies had not recommended jury trials for juvenile proceedings, and that the various state JJSs needed the freedom to experiment in their attempts to achieve the high promise of the JJS.

In *Kent* and *Gault* Mr. Justice Fortas had written majority opinions which revised fundamental premises of the JJS. No longer were juvenile court judges permitted to ignore procedural niceties in order to do what they thought best for the child. The Court had concluded that the JJS was incapable of matching action with rhetoric, largely because of the significant gap between social scientists' aspirations and abilities, and the apparent lack of funding and personnel to implement the social knowledge that was available. However, in the Burger dissent in *Winship* and the Blackmun plurality opinion in *McKeiver* we find a rekindling of faith in the ability of the JJS to achieve its goals. It seems reasonable to suggest that the JJS is now coming back to a middle ground between the socialized and the constitutionalized phases. The JJS of the late 1970s may be described most accurately as a synthesis of the two previous eras of the JJS:

Thus, in the space of six years, the United States Supreme Court had accepted the constitutionalist argument, had revised juvenile procedure and philosophy substantially, had seen the impact of its decisions minimized in practice, and had moved to mark the current limits of revision. The juvenile justice philosophy which has emerged from the constitutionalist revision is a synthesis of the socialized and constitutionalist positions. (Faust and Brantingham, 1974: 360)

Another phenomenon unique to the constitutionalized era is the emergence of an informal JJS existing parallel to and often in competition with the formal JJS. By the informal JJS is meant the collage of social service agencies which serve the young people of a community but which are not necessarily a regular part of the formal JJS. Such agencies are the recipients of referrals from formal JJS agencies and include youth service bureaus, drug abuse counselors, community mental health clinics, and regular probation officers acting in an unofficial capacity in supervising a child under "informal probation." The informal JJS performs all the same functions and tasks as the formal JJS but does so in a much less restricted, legalistic, and procedurally defined fashion. For example, the decision as to the truth of an allegation is not made by a judge in a courtroom after a hearing but is made by a probation officer or other counselor in a closed conference after a brief discussion. The choice of the most appropriate disposition for the child is made in a similar fashion. In many respects, the informal JJS affords the probation officer and other youth social workers the power and authority that was formerly theirs under the socialized JJS but was taken away by the constitutionalized JJS and given to the courts.

This latest era of the JJS might be described as a bifurcation of the JJS into formal and informal branches rather than a synthesis of socialized and constitutionalized positions (Shullenberger and Murphy, 1973). Many jurisdictions have formalized this bifurcation in legislation which channels the child who violates criminal laws into the formal system (police, courts, institutions) and the child whose delinquent acts are not criminal law violations into the informal system (school counselors, informal probation supervision, youth service bureaus) (Miller et al., 1971). Often the formal JJS serves as a backstop for the informal JJS, allowing system agents to threaten the child with being processed through the formal JJS if he doesn't "volunteer" for the informal JJS. The flow charts and discussion in chapter 5 will illustrate this phenomenon more fully; problems with the informal JJS will be discussed in chapter 7.

JJS AS A LEGAL SYSTEM FOR CHILDREN

From its beginning in 1899 the juvenile court has been a court of equity with administrative functions incidental to equity jursidiction (Ketcham and Paulsen, 1967). The first juvenile court was not a new and independent court but was simply one of several jursidictions of a general circuit court. As a court the juvenile court carries with it the aura and tradition of courts in the Anglo-American common law tradition. Juvenile court judges, prosecutors, defense counsel, and other court officers are not likely to forget they are in a courtroom, which puts definite limits upon the informality and procedural liberties so common in JJS rhetoric (Davis, 1974). Children and their parents may also feel the sense of dignity and "sacredness" found in our courtrooms. The wood paneling, judicial dais, and prominent flags present the unmistakable impression of the majesty of government. If the juvenile court were an administrative agency instead of a court, it would still have rules and regulations by which to operate but would not have that sense of awe that a courtroom and a judge tend to inspire.

All other functions and subsystems of the JJS are also, first and foremost, parts of a legal system, except those peripheral social service agencies making up the informal JJS or accepting referrals from a JJS agent (Murphy, 1974). For example, the policy/investigatory subsystem is operated primarily by sworn police officers and other police employees. This first JJS subsystem is so like the criminal justice system in its major functions as to render the differences more of academic curiosity than of practical importance. Police investigation of offenses, apprehension of juvenile suspects, questioning of juvenile suspects, examination of evidence, and other typical functions at this stage of the JJS are governed by legal rules and principles almost identical to those of the criminal justice system (Hahn, 1971), except that in some particulars the JJS is even more legally restrictive than the criminal justice system. For example, detention of a juvenile after apprehension but before appearance before a judicial officer may be more restricted for children than for adults in similar circumstances (no right to bail).

Like police and courts, the other stages and functions of the JJS are predominately those of a legal system quite like the criminal justice counterparts. Probation officers supervise an official, legally prescribed correctional program called probation. The rules of probation must be kept within legal limits, the power and authority of the probation officer is defined by statute and other primary sources of law, the rights of the probationer to receive treatment or reject profferred treatment are rights defined by law, and revocation of that probationary status can occur only after a legal hearing complete with evidence, witnesses, and lawyers (Klapmutz, 1972).

Juvenile institutions act in many ways like a social service agency but nevertheless are established by laws, restricted in their activities by laws, and required to provide certain services by law. The juvenile institution is no less a legalistic agency within a legal system than is a prison within the criminal justice system.

In addition to the impact of law and legal requirements on these particular JJS agencies, the fabric and aura of Anglo-American jurisprudence hangs over the JJS. As an example, consider the language from the United States Supreme Court:

...the admonition to function in a "parental" relationship is not an invitation to procedural arbitrariness. (*Kent*, at 555)

... we do hold that the [waiver] hearing must measure up to the essentials of due process and fair treatment. (*Kent*, at 562)

Due process of law is the primary and indispensable foundation of individual freedom. (*Gault*, at 20)

...the appearance as well as the actuality of fairness, impartiality and orderliness—in short, the essentials of due process—may be a more impressive and more therapeutic attitude so far as the juvenile is concerned. (*Gault*, at 26)

... civil labels and good intentions do not themselves obviate the need for criminal due process safeguards in juvenile courts.... (*Winship*, at 365–66).

The JJS is clearly a legal system governed by constitutions, statutes, and case law, and influenced by the long history of Anglo-American jurisprudence (Trojanowicz, 1973). Concurrently the JJS has been given a largely social service mission to accomplish. Let us now examine this dimension of the JJS.

JJS AS A SOCIAL WELFARE SYSTEM FOR CHILDREN

Although cloaked in the garb of an American legal system, the JJS is also a social welfare system (Tenney, 1969) in that it is a collection of private and public services attempting to ameliorate social pathology through a systematic method of adjusting an individual's relationships with other persons and with the wider social environment. Specifically, the JJS is a collection of youth-serving agencies, public and private, attempting to reduce juvenile delinquency through a system-like method of modifying the juvenile's behavior. Many prominent youth-serving agencies—for example, the Boy Scouts of America and the Young Men's Christian Association—are similar social welfare systems for children and differ from the JJS more in scope and reach than in purpose or goals.

Characterization of the JJS as more of a social welfare system than a legal system is not new or unorthodox:

> The theory of the District's Juvenile Court Act, like that of other jurisdictions, is rooted in social welfare philosophy rather than in the *corpus juris*. Its proceedings are designated as civil rather than criminal. The Juvenile Court is theoretically engaged in determining the needs of the child and of society rather than adjudicating criminal conduct. The objectives are to provide measures of guidance and rehabilitation for the child and protection for society, not to fix criminal responsibility, guilt and punishment. (*Kent*, at 554)

As a result of this fundamental social welfare premise, the "peculiar system for juveniles" (*Gault*, at 17) historically did not follow the traditional legal rules of criminal proceedings or even the much less demanding legal rules of civil proceedings (*Gault*, at 17, fn. 22). JJS agents were not trying to punish or seek revenge upon the child but were simply trying to provide proper parental custody and protection (Edwards, 1971). They saw themselves, and still tend to see themselves, as comparable to the laudable social worker who discovers an abandoned baby on the front stoop and takes in the perishable foundling to provide it with food, clothing, shelter, and the multitude of other ministrations needed by such an infant. Suggesting that such a servant of humanity should be restricted in providing this essential rescue or should have to prove in a court (beyond a reasonable doubt) that the foundling needs such rescue would test the limits of community tolerance. To suggest that the abandoned baby has a right to remain on the front stoop unbothered by over-eager governmental agents is to blaspheme conventional common sense (Brennan and Klinduka, 1970).

As extreme as the above example is, it reveals the ramifications of the social welfare characteristics of the JJS. We may punish persons only reluctantly and only after we are sure that we must. We may help persons eagerly and do not wait until we are absolutely certain of their need. Therefore, the criminal justice system may be considered to be rational as an admittedly punishing system which requires procedural patience and a high degree of certainty before administering the punishment. However, the JJS may seem irrational because it also requires procedural patience and a high degree of certainty before we can help a needy child.

Consider language from our Supreme Court justices:

In a criminal case, on the other hand, we do not view the social disutility of convicting an innocent man as equivalent to the disutility of acquitting someone who is guilty.... In this context, I view the requirement of proof beyond a reasonable doubt in a criminal case as bottomed on a fundamental value determination of our society that it is far worse to convict an innocent man than to let a guilty man go free. (Mr. Justice Harlan, concurring in *Winship*, at 372)

... a declaration of delinquency "*is* significantly different from and less onerous than a finding of criminal guilt...." (Mr. Justice Blackmun, in *McKeiver*, at 540, quoting the lower court majority opinion)

If the formalities of the criminal adjudicative process are to be superimposed upon the juvenile court system, there is little need for a separate existence. Perhaps that ultimate disillusionment will come one day, but for the moment we are disinclined to give impetus to it. (Mr. Justice Blackmun, in *McKeiver*, at 551)

The United States Supreme Court—that ultimate guardian and standard setter for legal systems—accepts the fact that the JJS is not yet a purely legal system comparable to the criminal justice system. As a helping, proactive, social welfare system, the JJS is given as much legal freedom as can be tolerated and still remain within the family of legal systems. The JJS is more accurately described as existing in that uncertain overlap area between the intersecting circles of legal systems and social welfare systems. Of course, all legal systems are partly social welfare systems and vice versa, but the JJS seems to straddle that centermost demarcation between the two.

GOALS, OBJECTIVES, AND OPERATING PRINCIPLES OF THE JJS

The JJS has been burdened with often unrealistic goals and objectives. In a very real sense, the JJS is asked to do what the child's parents, local community, school system, etc., have not been able to do. The JJS is to seek the same goals and objectives as "good, American parents" would for their child (Edwards, 1971). It is not simply to seek punishment for the child.

The Juvenile Court is theoretically engaged in determining the needs of the child and of society rather than adjudicating criminal conduct. The objectives are to provide measures of guidance and rehabilitation for the child and protection for society, not to fix criminal responsibility, guilt and punishment. The State is *parens patriae* rather than prosecuting attorney and judge. (*Kent*, at 554–55)

Indeed, rehabilitation of the child is the predominant goal of the entire JJS (President's Commission, 1967: 80). Obviously, society is best protected from future delinquent behavior from a child if that child is rehabilitated and thus engages in no further delinquent behavior. Our society has also assumed, apparently without argument, that the child is best served by the JJS if he is taught to avoid delinquent behavior in the future. Thus, rehabilitation of the child serves the two masters of the JJS: the best interests of the child and the best interests of society.

Moving from the child to children and from the delinquent to delinquency, the JJS also has the goal of generally deterring delinquency among all children by its very existence and ability to act. To deter effectively, the JJS should be characterized by thorough investigation of delinquent acts, swift apprehension of delinquent children, prompt and accurate adjudication of facts, and imposition of just dispositions (President's Commission, 1967: 88).

Operating principles of the JJS include those inherited from law, those inherited from social service, and those required by the practicalities of governmental operations. American legal concepts require the JJS to follow the precepts of the Bill of Rights and the Fourteenth Amendment (*Kent* and *Gault*). These legal operating principles are today very much like the operating principles of the American criminal justice system, particularly in such specifics as the right to counsel, right to notice, right to proof beyond a reasonable doubt, right to fair evidentiary hearings, etc. (Fox, 1972).

Operating principles inherited from the social service origins of the JJS require it to serve the needs of its clientele. Thus, the JJS must determine the needs of the particular child in question and do its best to serve those needs. Likewise, the needs of the society it serves must be determined and met to the extent possible (Tenney, 1969).

The practicalities of governmental operations dictate that the JJS live within reasonable budgets, hire agents from the available pool of candidates, treat delinquent children with therapeutic skills limited by man's knowledge, and operate within the vagaries of modern society. Thus, the legal and social service exhortations concerning rehabilitation of the delinquent child may often be negated by the practical reality of limited financial resources or, more fatally, by the present lack of socio-psycho-medical knowledge. Regardless of the ringing goals, objectives, and operating principles of the legal scholars and social service theorists, the JJS must deal with real, living children who live in a real world.

3. FUNCTIONAL DESCRIPTION AND ANALYSIS OF THE JJS

As expounded above, the JJS is a legal system based upon American concepts of law as well as a social welfare system based upon concepts of serving the needs of a certain group of people. This section describes in some detail the functions typically performed within the JJS and discusses the need for these functions as well as the possibility of changing or eliminating some of them. The charts and verbal descriptions which follow represent the JJS as it operates in most jurisdictions today. Of course, minor variations occur frequently. However, the basic system presented herein is the JJS as it typically exists or at least as our laws and agency policies require it to exist. Where current practice markedly deviates from the required system, this is described.

CONCEPT OF THE JJS AS A SYSTEM

The popularity of the phrases "criminal justice *system*," "welfare *system*," and "juvenile justice *system*" may have caused many of us to accept too readily the term "system" without seriously questioning its meaning or appropriateness. Perhaps like the terms "love," "peace," "great," "brilliant," and "*gentle*man," it is heard so often that we accept it uncritically. Conversely, it has become fashionable to refer to the JJS as being so unsystematic as to be a nonsystem (Coffey, 1974: 43). Thus, the JJS *as a system* must be understood.

The juvenile justice system is clearly a system, albeit a poorly functioning system and one that has suffered from lack of attention to system design and engineering. The following general comment about systems seems appropriate in the juvenile justice context:

> . . . any time we assemble people and things and arrange for them to go about performing a task, we have "designed" a system. It may be an abysmally inferior system. The system's engineering may be rated as of low quality, in some instances hardly recognizable as engineering. But it is still a system. (Ramo, 1969: 29)

In the instance of the JJS, our law-making bodies have through their various enactments and decisions "designed" the JJS by assembling people,

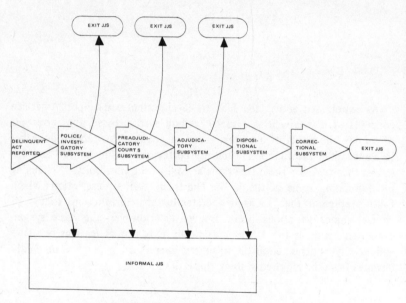

FIGURE 1. SUBSYSTEMS WITHIN THE JJS

agencies, and other "things" to go about performing the task of processing children designated as in need of their services. The "design" of the JJS has been further refined by courts, agency policy, routinized procedures, personal value systems, and a myriad other factors.

The JJS includes and actually begins with the legislative enactments and court decisions which establish and modify the rules by which the system operates. The JJS also includes the police agencies and personnel which often are the child's first contact with the JJS. The JJS includes the juvenile courts and probation offices, which normally are the power center of the JJS. The JJS includes all the social service agencies surrounding the legal system, which increasingly are becoming an alternative to the legalistic juvenile court subsystem. The JJS, finally, includes the juvenile correctional subsystem with its many innovative alternatives. Figure 1 illustrates the basic configuration of the various subsystems within the JJS and the informal JJS.

All these subsystems within the JJS actually operate as somewhat independent systems themselves. It is the relative independence of these JJS subsystems, such as the police agencies and the juvenile institutions, from the rest of the JJS that can be a major source of counterproductivity and conflicting attitudes within the JJS (Kratcoski and Hernandez, 1974).

Each subsystem, agency, and agent within the JJS should be working toward the same goals and be working under the same operating principles. In the following functional analysis this will be assumed, and contrary indications will be pointed out as countersystem activities. However, the JJS lacks one essential element for it to function as a system: a true system manager. No one agent or agency has exercised power effective to control the activities of the other agents and agencies within the JJS. For example, if an automobile is operating in an undesirable manner, the driver has effective power to control the automobile's activities (steering, accelerator, brakes, etc.). If the power is ineffective, an automobile mechanic can modify the automobile's parts and subsystems so as to make it perform correctly. As another example, consider the production line in a manufacturing enterprise. The production line foreman has effective power to modify and control the various human and nonhuman elements so as to make the production line perform correctly. If a machine is operated incorrectly, the worker may be retrained, redirected, or replaced. If the entire production line seems to be faulty, a production engineer is called in to redesign it. Consider the management headaches which would result if the production line foreman or some management official did not exercise ultimate effective power to control the activities of the production system. Consider your frustration with your automobile if neither you nor the automotive mechanic had effective power to control its speed. Perhaps now we can understand the problems of a system without a system manager. Such is the JJS.

The fact that the JJS is an American legal system, similar to the American criminal justice system, makes it impossible for it to have a true system manager. The JJS was designed largely by the legislative branch of government, is dominated in the first subsystem by agents and agencies within the executive branch of the government (primarily police agencies), passes through central subsystems controlled by the judicial branch of the government (juvenile courts and probation officers), and as a last resort terminates back in the executive branch of the government (juvenile state institutions). A fundamental premise of our governmental system is that the three branches of government remain separate but equal, with none having direct supervisory control over the other. The only minor exception to this fundamental premise is the somewhat domineering power of courts to control legal systems. However, as will be made clearer in subsequent sections, regardless of the court's proclamations other agencies and agents within the JJS remain fairly independent and uncontrolled (Eldefonso and Coffey, 1976).

Thus, the JJS is a system and can be analyzed as a system. However, the JJS is destined to remain a relatively inefficient system for which being "out of control" is standard operating procedure.

POLICE/INVESTIGATORY SUBSYSTEM OF THE JJS

Figure 2 illustrates this first JJS subsystem by a simplistic flow diagram, identifying the major functions and decision points. Although usually the first JJS event is the police department's receipt of a report of an incident which turns out to be an act of delinquency (Flammang, 1972), previous non-JJS events have a significant impact on the JJS. Since we are assuming in the JJS analysis that the child is being processed as a suspected delinquent, a critical pre-JJS event is the occurrence of an act of delinquency. In theory at least, the JJS is never activated unless and until an act of delinquency is committed.

This JJS subsystem does not include the commission of an act of delinquency as taking place within the JJS but the JJS does have an impact on that event. In any given case, a child may be specifically deterred from committing an act of delinquency because of the mere existence of the JJS. Or, the child may modify the kind of act of delinquency committed (such as joyriding instead of automobile theft) because of the anticipated reaction of the JJS. Perhaps the child will take elaborate pains to cover up the act of delinquency or to lie about its occurrence, because of the JJS. Thus, although the occurrence of an act of delinquency is not technically a part of this subsystem or of the JJS, it does have a significant impact upon the JJS and the JJS may have a significant impact upon it. Moreover, if this event never occurred there would be no need for the JJS.

A subsequent and almost as important an event is the discovery of the occurrence of the delinquent act by someone in a position to report the act to an official of the JJS. For example, if a child shoplifts and is not discovered by the store owner, the parent, or someone else, the act of delinquency will in all probability never be reported to a JJS official.

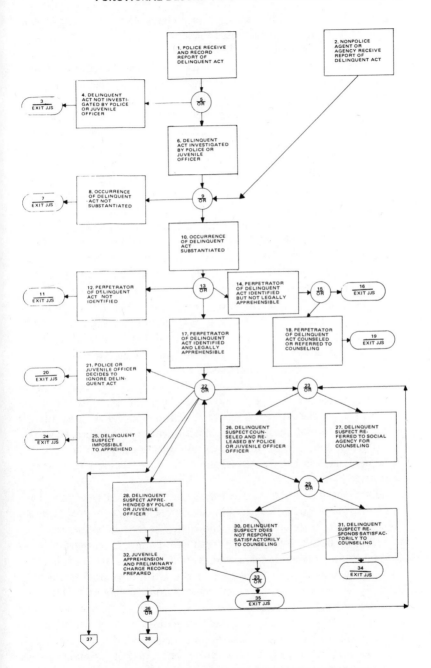

FIGURE 2. POLICE/INVESTIGATORY SUBSYSTEM OF THE JJS

If a child burglarizes a home and is very clever about it, taking only a few items that would not be missed for some time, the act of delinquency may never be reported. If a fourteen-year-old boy forcibly rapes his thirteen-year-old girl friend after an established sexual relationship with her over a period of time, the probability of this act of delinquency ever being reported is very low. In sum, the delinquent act may never be discovered or the persons aware of the occurrence of the act of delinquency may not be in a position to report it. Either way, this first activating event in the JJS never occurs.

For the sake of our analysis, let us assume that an act of delinquency has occurred and that the occurrence of that act of delinquency is known to someone in a position to report it to a JJS official. The first actual JJS event occurs when that act of delinquency is reported to a police or other JJS agency which can receive such reports. Typically, the report will be received by the police agency (figure 2, function 1). If the report is received by another JJS agency (figure 2, function 2), typically that agency will question the reporter and examine other evidence to determine if the report is apparently valid (figure 2, "or" gate 9). If the police receive the report (figure 2, function 1), they may or may not investigate in any significant manner (figure 2, "or" gate 5) (Eldefonso, 1972). For example, if the police receive a report from a local merchant that someone ("probably some kid") has shoplifted a carton of cigarettes but the merchant doesn't know when it happened, who did it, or where the cigarettes and the alleged delinquent might be by now, the police will most probably do no more than record the report/complaint and agree to notify the merchant if the merchandise is recovered. The delinquent act, even though it did occur, is not meaningfully investigated by the police (figure 2, function 4), and, barring unusual events, the actual perpetrator of the delinquent act will exit the JJS (figure 2, terminal 3) before really having got started in it.

So far this analysis of the JJS events and functions may seem to have belabored the obvious. However, it is significant that the number of actual perpetrators of delinquent acts who never have their delinquent acts reported or have them reported with grossly insufficient information far exceed the number of them who make it past the preliminary hurdles. The critical importance of this fact to the JJS is obvious. Regardless of carefully conceived treatment and rehabilitation programs for children who commit delinquent acts, we never specifically identify the majority of these children. Indeed, it could be argued that the percentage of children who actually commit delinquent acts is nearly 100 percent. It is apparently common for professors who teach juvenile delinquency and juvenile justice courses to ask the entering students to enumerate the kinds of acts of delinquency they perpetrated as children. Few of us have had students who have handed in a clean sheet. However, some children do enter the JJS for having committed the same acts of delinquency that the rest of us did as children. This selection process may tend to discriminate against certain groups of children (Ferdinand and Luchterband, 1970).

Let us assume now that our hypothetical delinquent has made it to the point that the reported delinquent act is investigated by the police or juvenile officer (figure 2, function 6) (Flammang, 1973). The nature of the act reported may well determine who the investigator will be. If the police agency receives a report of a house burglary, it will investigate the alleged burglary in the same manner regardless of whether it is legally a crime (committed by an adult) or an act of delinquency (committed by a child) (Weston and Wells, 1974). The act is the same for investigative purposes, at least in deciding whether or not a burglary has indeed occurred (figure 2, "or" gate 9). If the police report indicates that the alleged incident is a fairly common juvenile act, such as school vandalism, then the investigator may be able to assume from the beginning that the incident being investigated is legally an act of delinquency instead of a crime (Eldefonso, 1972; Flammang, 1972).

If the police investigation does not reveal sufficient evidence to establish that a crime or act of delinquency has probably occurred (figure 2, function 8), generally the case will be dismissed and our hypothetical perpetrator will exit the JJS (figure 2, terminal 7). If the investigation substantiates the fact that an act of delinquency has occurred (figure 2, function 10), the investigation moves on to establish the identity of the perpetrator of the delinquent act (figure 2, "or" gate 13) (Eldefonso, 1973).

If the perpetrator of the delinquent act is not identified as a result of the investigation (figure 2, function 12), the case is closed and the perpetrator exits the JJS (figure 2, terminal 11). If the perpetrator of the delinquent act is identified by the police investigation but the identifying evidence falls short of sufficient evidence ("probable cause") to apprehend and take into custody the perpetrator of the act of delinquency (figure 2, function 14), two primary options present themselves (figure 2, "or" gate 15). The perpetrator of the act of delinquency can simply exit the JJS (figure 2, terminal 16). More likely, he will be counseled by the police and/or referred to some social service agency for counseling (figure 2, function 18) and then released from the JJS (figure 2, terminal 19) (Pursuit, 1972). This second route (functions 18–19) is not based upon any legal coercion or threat of bringing the child into court, as is typically the case when a child is encouraged to seek counseling at subsequent points in the JJS (Sundeen, 1972). In this situation the counseling agent has no "enforcer" of his recommendations to the child, and thus the attempts at counseling in this configuration must depend upon the sincere desire of the child and his parents to be rehabilitated. Predictably, these instances are rare. Most often this unprovable act of delinquency is simply remembered by police officials and used to justify more legalistic, less informal handling of a subsequent provable offense by this child. The informal JJS is discussed in more detail in chapter 7 below.

If the perpetrator of the act of delinquency is identified by the investigation and sufficient evidence ("probable cause") has been uncovered to take the child into custody (figure 2, function 17), the police and other juvenile officials face a multi-option decision point (figure 2, "or" gate 22). A somewhat unlikely but possible option would be for the police or juvenile officer simply to ignore the delinquent act (figure 2, function 21) and permit the perpetrator to exit the JJS (figure 2, terminal 20). For example, this could happen when a police officer observes a child loitering in a public place after the legal curfew hour. The officer reports the act (mentally to himself), and he investigates the report (notes the age of the child and checks his watch for the correct time). He has substantiated the occurrence of the act of delinquency, identified the perpetrator of the delinquent act, and has sufficient evidence to apprehend the child. However, the officer decides to ignore the delinquent act and not even mention it to the perpetrator, for one or more of many reasons: The officer is tired and wants to get back to the station; he thinks the curfew laws are too strict; the child is known to him as a "good kid" who doesn't get into trouble; he is staked out for a major narcotics investigation and doesn't want to reveal his identity; etc. (Newman, 1968). In another case, the officer finds the perpetrator of the delinquent act impossible to apprehend (figure 2, function 25) and closes the case (figure 2, terminal 24). This could occur when the child dies during a violent encounter following an armed robbery or when the child's escape and subsequent runaway/disappearance is so effective that he is never located by the police.

The police may decide that the child should not be apprehended and/or referred on to juvenile court but instead should be shunted into the juvenile justice limbo referred to by several vague, euphemistic terms. For our purposes we shall refer to this as the "informal JJS." This informal JJS will be described at length later because it is most commonly activated as a result of the decision of a court intake screening officer in lieu of filing a formal court petition. However, the child may be shunted into the informal JJS by the individual police officer or by the police agency, typically acting through the juvenile division of the police agency,

(Statton, 1974). The police officer could activate the informal JJS by referring the child to a social agency for counseling (figure 2, function 27), or (figure 2, "or" gate 23) by giving the child "a good talking to" like a stern father (figure 2, function 26). Then the officer may generally observe his behavior for some time thereafter and as a result decide whether or not the child has benefited from the counseling (figure 2, "or" gate 29). If the child seems to have responded favorably (figure 2, function 31), the previous delinquent act is forgiven and the child exits the JJS (figure 2, terminal 34). If the child does not seem to have responded favorably to counseling (figure 2, function 30), the officer must decide (figure 2, "or" gate 33) whether simply to forget about the case (figure 2, terminal 35) or to consider some other possible option (figure 2, "or" gate 22) (Somerville, 1969).

This informal treatment of the child by an individual police officer may be most frequent in the small town situation where regular surveillance of the local children is an almost daily occurrence. In such a situation the individual officer may be more prone to act as a big brother or surrogate father to the child as compared to the officer in a more impersonal large city where such attitudes may be less prevalent. The propensity for this kind of "personal adjustment" of a delinquency case also varies greatly between individual officers and between police agencies (Kobetz, 1971).

The police officer may decide that the case should be referred to juvenile court before the child is apprehended (figure 2, connector 37). The next step in the JJS for this child will be the juvenile court intake screening procedures (figure 3, function 45). This avoidance of apprehension and detention may occur in a situation in which the child admits his involvement in nonserious criminal acts and shows no indication of being a threat to the community or of running away from the authorities. Even if the police officer nevertheless believes that court action is necessary, the officer could justifiably conclude that apprehension and detention would be superfluous (Davis, 1971).

The final option open to the police officer would be to apprehend the delinquent and take him into custody (figure 2, function 28) (Klein et al., 1975). Following apprehension and transporting the child to a police station, a juvenile "booking" procedure is followed in which the apprehension is recorded and preliminary charge records are prepared (figure 2, function 32) (Juvenile Police, 1972; Vandiver, 1970). Following the records preparation process, the police agency must then decide (figure 2, "or" gate 36) whether to refer the child on to juvenile court (figure 2, connector 38) or to shunt him into the informal JJS (figure 2, "or" gate 23). This latter process, often referred to as "station adjustment" (President's

Commission, 1967: 82-83), occurs when the decision to take responsibility for counseling a child takes place at the police station as a result of an agency deliberation. In this mode, the perpetrator of the delinquent act follows the same sequence as when the individual police officer decides to counsel and monitor the child. It is not unusual for station adjustments to involve rather elaborate hearings and the imposition of "sanctions" by the police agency (Juvenile, 1966: 776-85). This usurpation of the overall responsibility of the entire JJS has been soundly criticized (President's Commission, 1967: 83) and seems to be quite unnecessary. See chapter 5, recommendation 9, for a further discussion of this situation.

If the child is intensively questioned or interrogated by the police, this commonly occurs after apprehension and before referral to juvenile court intake. Any questioning—particularly interrogation—of a child is fraught with difficulties and is simplified legally if the child's parents are present (Allman, 1972; Saylor, 1973). Children's protection against aggressive interrogation is increasing (Shoben, 1973). The degree to which police rely on interrogation of juveniles varies widely among police agencies (Ferster and Courtless, 1969).

The police/investigatory subsystem of the JJS has now completed its functions. The perpetrator of the delinquent act has either exited the JJS (the result for a vast majority of them) or has been referred on to subsequent subsystems of the JJS. Two characteristics of this subsystem stand out. First, the police/investigatory subsystem serves as a screening device for children entering the JJS. Of all children who commit delinquent acts, only a very few enter the JJS. Of those children who do enter the JJS (as described in this subsystem), even fewer are referred on to subsequent subsystems of the JJS. As was illustrated in the discussion of the early stages of this subsystem, this screening tendency results in few actually delinquent children being subject to the therapeutic functions of the JJS. Thus, can society realistically ask the JJS to deal effectively with juvenile delinquency when such a small percentage of actual delinquents are processed by it to any significant extent?

PREADJUDICATORY COURT SUBSYSTEM OF THE JJS

Just as the police/investigatory subsystem of the JJS is almost totally controlled and performed by police officers and agencies, the preadjudicatory court subsystem is almost totally controlled and performed by juvenile court personnel. This JJS subsystem inherits the child from the control of the police and either dismisses him entirely, shunts him off into the informal JJS, transfers him to criminal court, or sends him on into the juvenile court's adjudicatory hearing (see figure 3). Although glancing through figure 3 might lead one to conclude that the key persons are the juvenile court judge and prosecutor, it will become obvious that the primary power center in this JJS subsystem, and probably the entire JJS, is the juvenile probation officer.

Input for this subsystem comes from referral from police officers either after the delinquent has been apprehended (figure 3, connector 38) or after a decision not to apprehend him (figure 3, connector 37). Obviously, if the child is not apprehended before being referred to juvenile court intake screening hearings (figure 3, connector 37), no detention/ release problem arises, and the next JJS function is the screening hearing (figure 3, function 45). However, if the delinquent is apprehended and taken into police custody, a decision must be made as to if and when that custody should be terminated pending further proceedings (Ferster et al., 1969; Peterson, 1972). This decision is usually made by a juvenile court probation officer acting through the authority of the juvenile court judge (figure 3, function 39). The decision (figure 3, "or" gate 40) is whether to release the delinquent pending further proceedings (figure 3, function 42) or to detain him (figure 3, function 41) (McLean, 1969).

If the probation officer's decision is to detain the child, as soon as possible the juvenile court must afford the incarcerated child a hearing to establish the legality and appropriateness of the detention (figure 3, function 44) (Simms, 1972; Drinan, 1969). As a result of that hearing the juvenile court judge may decide (figure 3, "or" gate 43) either to release the child from detention (figure 3, function 42) or to continue the detention and proceed to the intake screening hearing (figure 3, function 45) (Hammergren, 1973).

The decision to detain a child in some form of juvenile detention center is not to be taken lightly (Sumner, 1971). While typically less lethargic than criminal proceedings, the adjudicatory hearing and formal JJS decisions about the child's legal complicity in delinquent behavior may take several weeks or months (Steketee, 1969). Meanwhile the child is missing school, perhaps a part-time job, family life, peer group involvement, etc. (Mora, 1969). On the other hand, if the child has demonstrated serious antisocial tendencies, particularly of a violent, destructive nature, society has a valid interest in being protected from such a person, child or not, while preparations for the adjudicatory hearing are being made. Juvenile court statutes most often reveal a clear preference for release of the child (to his parents if possible) unless the child presents a clear threat to the community or clearly indicates a probability that he will not appear for subsequent proceedings (Miller et al., 1971: 1266–86; O'Rourke and Salem, 1968). This release to parents is in lieu of a right

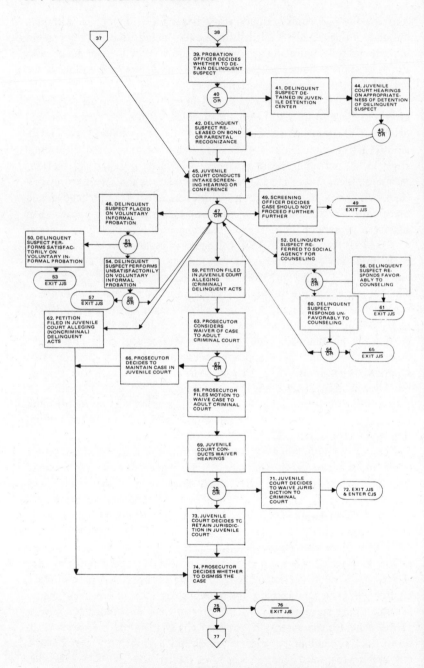

FIGURE 3. PREADJUDICATORY COURT SUBSYSTEM OF THE JJS

to bail (Kalnins, 1971; Smith, 1971). Note also that many "juvenile detention centers" are either simply an isolated cell in the local jail or are so like a jail as to make the euphemistic name a sick joke (Sarri, 1973). Such short-term incarceration facilities are widely recognized as very inappropriate places to house children and almost certain to worsen whatever behavior problems the child might have upon entry. The decision to detain a child pending further proceedings can in many cases result in such a negative impact upon him as to render ineffectual the post-detention attempts to rehabilitate him. Many communities have developed alternatives to detention (Ariessohn and Closson, 1971).

Whether detained or released, the suspect's next step is to submit to the intake screening hearing or conference (figure 3, function 45) (Palmier, 1968; Ralston, 1971). The intake counselor or hearing officer should evaluate cases received on three primary bases (Johnson, 1975: 80):

1. Is the complaint one in which the juvenile court has proper jurisdiction?

2. Is there sufficient evidence to support the allegations of the complaint?

3. Will the situation best be addressed through an informal process or by filing a petition for formal action?

The actual bases for an intake counselor's decisions may vary somewhat from the ideal (Thomas and Sieverdes, 1975; Weiner and Willie, 1971). In making the screening decision (figure 3, "or" gate 47), the decision maker has three basic alternatives: the delinquent can be released from the JJS, handled informally by the probation office or other social service agency, or sent into juvenile court via the filing of a formal petition (Terry, 1967). This screening decision is likely to be made following one or more informal conferences or hearings involving the intake officer, the delinquent, and his parents (Miller, 1971: 1262-66). Although the screening officer is the primary decision maker, the prosecutor (Youthful, 1973) and defense attorney (Reinhold, 1968) may be involved also.

It is entirely possible that the screening officer will decide that the case should not proceed any further (figure 3, function 48); then the delinquent will exit the JJS (figure 3, terminal 49). For example, consider a situation in which a child runs away from home and is referred to the intake screening hearing. Meanwhile the child returns home and all is forgiven when the child convincingly swears never to do it again. It would be quite common, and in concert with the goals and operating principles of the JJS, for the screening officer to dismiss the case. In fact, for the screening officer to refer such a case on to juvenile court would seem to be in clear conflict with the goals and operating principles of the JJS (Ferster and Courtless, 1971).

Even if the screening officer does not dismiss the case outright, it is still possible, even probable, that the case will not proceed to the filing of a formal court petition alleging delinquent behavior (Croxton, 1967). The case can be handled informally in two ways, either of which is a means of utilizing the informal JJS (Ferster et al., 1970). The screening officer can refer the child to a social service agency such as a Youth Services Bureau for counseling and whatever other services may be required (figure 3, function 52) (Sherwood, 1972). Many communities have developed inventive alternative programs (Austin and Speidel, 1971; Morris, 1970). If that referral produces favorable results (figure 3, function 56), the child will exit the JJS (figure 3, terminal 61). Whether or not the referral results are favorable (figure 3, "or" gate 55) is a decision normally made by the screening officer at a subsequent time, with the help of information from the social service agency to which the child was referred. If the child does not respond favorably to counseling (figure 3, function 60), the screening officer or comparable JJS agent must decide (figure 3, "or" gate 64) whether the case should be reconsidered. If no apparent value would result from such a reconsideration, the child can exit from the JJS (figure 3, terminal 65). The alternative would be to "rescreen" the case to determine if another alternative would be more appropriate (figure 3, "or" gate 47).

The other means of handling the case informally would be to place the child on voluntary informal probation. As with the above informal channel, satisfactory performance on voluntary informal probation (figure 3, function 50) will result in a termination of activity by the JJS (figure 3, terminal 53). The alternative (figure 3, "or" gate 51) for unsatisfactory performance by the child (figure 3, function 54) can be either to exit the JJS (figure 3, terminal 57) or (figure 3, "or" gate 58) to return to another alternative (figure 3, "or" gate 47).

If the case were to proceed on through juvenile court hearings, the most probable formal dispositional alternative would be formal probation (Schwarzenberger, 1971). By encouraging the child to "volunteer" for informal probation, almost exactly the same result is achieved and without the time, expense, and uncertainty of juvenile court hearings. Thus, a juvenile justice disposition is imposed upon the child, albeit informally and without a juvenile court record, and the state has significantly intervened in the child's life without following any requirements of due process or fundamental fairness. It is by the "threat" of formal court action that voluntary compliance with informal probation is achieved. In effect, the power of the informal JJS to function is based upon the threat of resort to the formal JJS.

If outright release or informal diversion is not chosen by the screening officer, the "last resort" (President's Commission, 1967: 80-81) is the filing of a petition in juvenile court formally alleging delinquent acts. The petition can be filed by a police officer, probation officer, parent, victim, or any other reputable adult (Besharov, 1974: 189-90). The functions served by the petition are to describe the alleged facts, present arguments why the court has jurisdiction and venue over the case, and apprise the child respondent and his parents so that a defense can be prepared (Besharov, 1974: 190; Ritter, 1968).

The particular route is determined by whether the petition alleges delinquent acts which would be criminal acts if committed by an adult (figure 3, function 59) or delinquent acts which are not criminal acts, such as truancy, habitual disobedience, etc. (figure 3, function 62). If the petition alleges noncriminal acts of delinquency, waiver to criminal court is impossible since the criminal court could have no jurisdiction over non-criminal acts (Alers, 1973). Thus, the next step would be the prosecutor's consideration of the prosecutive merit of the case and whether the case should be dismissed (figure 3, function 74).

If the petition alleges acts of delinquency which would be criminal if committed by an adult, the prosecutor routinely considers whether or not to seek to transfer the case to criminal court (figure 3, "or" gate 67) (Zekas, 1973). If the prosecutor decides to maintain the case in juvenile court (figure 3, function 66), the case will then be handled in the same manner as a case involving noncriminal allegations. If the decision is made to seek waiver or transfer of the case (figure 3, function 68), then the case moves to a waiver hearing conducted by the juvenile court (figure 3, function 69) (Garner, 1973). Although this decision of whether or not to seek waiver of a juvenile case to criminal court obviously involves the prosecutor in a critical way, the initial decision can be made by the person who filed the petition, such as a police officer, probation officer, or other juvenile justice official. The juvenile court judge can be the initiator of the decision to consider waiver, or the delinquent respondent may seek waiver, although the latter would be most unusual. The reasons for seeking such a waiver would be similar to the valid reasons for granting a waiver after the hearing; these reasons are discussed below. Another reason, more political than fitting to juvenile justice goals, would be to satisfy public indignation and the "cry for blood" after a particularly sensational crime played up in a spectacular fashion by the local news media.

If the prosecutor and/or other juvenile justice official does decide to seek waiver to criminal court (figure 3, function 68), the juvenile court must hold an appropriate waiver hearing (figure 3, function 69) (Burd, 1970). *Kent v. United States* establishes this requirement. Of the many JJS hearings and conferences, the waiver hearing, along with the adjudicatory hearing and the disposition hearing, is of highest importance. It is basically similar to other American adversary legal hearings in that the state presents evidence why the case should be transferred, the child respondent presents evidence why the case should be retained in juvenile court (Merz, 1968), and the judge makes findings of fact, arrives at a decision, and explains his reasons for his decision (Schornhorst, 1968). Among generally accepted valid reasons for deciding to waive a juvenile case to criminal court are:

1. the seriousness of the alleged offense and whether it involved personal violence;
2. the age, sophistication, and maturity of the child respondent;
3. the juvenile record and social history of the child respondent; and
4. the apparent ability of the JJS correctional subsystems to rehabilitate the child while protecting the general public.

Of course, the decision to waive is appealable and/or challengeable in subsequent criminal proceedings. However, the juvenile court's decision (figure 3, "or" gate 70) to waive the case to criminal court (figure 3, function 71) means for the purposes of this analysis that the child respondent exits the JJS (figure 3, terminal 72).

If the juvenile court judge decides to retain jurisdiction of the case within the JJS (figure 3, function 73), the next step is the prosecutor's determination of whether or not to proceed with the case (figure 3, function 73). Of course, if the prosecutor or other person pushing the case decides (figure 3, "or" gate 75) to dismiss it, the child respondent exits the JJS (figure 3, terminal 76). If the case is not dismissed at this point, it moves on to the adjudicatory court subsystem of the JJS (figure 3, connector 77).

ADJUDICATORY COURT SUBSYSTEM OF THE JJS

If a child respondent enters this subsystem of the JJS, the decision has previously been made by an authorized JJS official to bring this case to court and to seek a formal adjudication. Typically, the only reason the child respondent might exit the JJS from this subsystem is insufficiency of evidence. The adjudicatory hearing is the focal point of this subsystem, and the juvenile court judge's final decision as to the child's legally delinquent status is the primary end result.

The case enters the adjudicatory court subsystem (figure 4, connector 77) at a point in the process after JJS officials have decided to press forward with the case and before the preadjudicatory hearing activities. Plea bargaining or response negotiation (figure 4, function 78) in the juvenile justice context tends to occur most commonly at this juncture, but the entire JJS can be viewed as one continuous bargaining process. When the child is first approached by a police officer, the bargaining begins and the child's ability to offer the proper bargaining position (apologetic, respectful, humble, and resolved never to do it again) determines largely whether the case will progress further. The child's bargaining posture at the police station, at the intake screening hearing, and at numerous other JJS junctures is a key determinant of the way his case is handled. It is clearly a "bargain" when the child agrees to undergo personal and family counseling and to accept special tutoring in return for not having a formal court petition filed against him.

This function (figure 4, function 78) is quite similar to the criminal justice counterpart in that it is truly a negotiation as to what response the delinquent respondent will make to the petition and what disposition will be recommended by the JJS officials at the disposition hearing (Gough, 1971b). As in the criminal justice counterpart, the delinquent respondent may offer to admit less serious allegations in return for a promise to drop more serious charges and to recommend a less restrictive dispositional alternative (Greenberg, 1972). Regardless of the juvenile justice rhetoric about matching the individual child's needs with the most appropriate dispositional alternative, the delinquent respondent typically desires the least interference and interruption in his life from the disposition and thus seeks probation instead of institutionalization, his present living situation instead of a group foster home, and similar choices. Of course, there are exceptions to this general rule, but there are few children, delinquent or not, that voluntarily seek a restrictive, somewhat punitive, living situation. Thus, traditional criminal justice plea bargaining, more appropriately "response negotiation" using JJS terminology, is a significant part of the juvenile justice process (Besharov, 1974: 311).

Following the response negotiation is the arraignment, conducted by the juvenile court judge (figure 4, function 79). At the arraignment the court considers the legal sufficiency of the petition, advises the delinquent respondent and his family of their legal rights, and accepts the respondent's response to the petition, plus some other legal functions not of importance here. Although dismissal of the case is a possible result of the arraignment, it is quite uncommon (Besharov, 1974: 228). Most frequently the arraigning judge's actions (figure 4, "or" gate 81) are determined by the respondent's reply to the allegations in the formal court petition. If the respondent admits the allegations made in the petition (figure 4, function 80), the adjudicatory hearing is bypassed and the process skips to the judge's decision to enter or withhold judgment (figure 4, "or" gate 96). If the respondent denies the allegations in the petition (figure 4, function 82), the case will move on to the adjudicatory hearing. In the latter

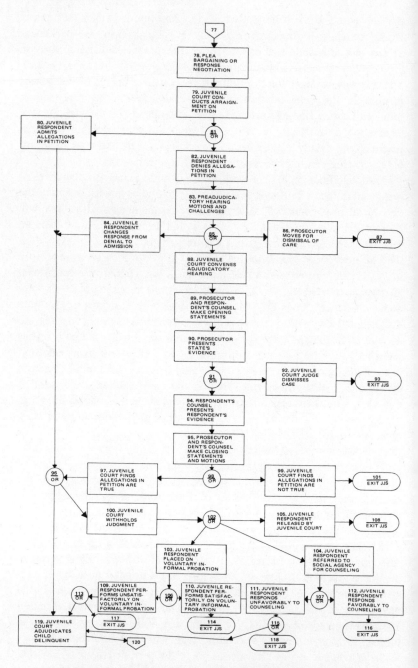

FIGURE 4. ADJUDICATORY COURT SUBSYSTEM OF THE JJS

option, the next step would be the preadjudicatory hearing motions and challenges (figure 4, function 83).

These prehearing motions and challenges can rely on civil or criminal law rules and will as a rule be addressed to the wording of the petition, to evidence or activities needed before the hearing begins (McGuire, 1973), to the actual conduct of the hearings, and/or to termination of the court proceedings (Besharov, 1974: 265-67). While this JJS analysis cannot go into the details of these legal maneuvers, it is important to appreciate the impact such motions can have on subsequent proceedings. For instance, consider a situation in which the prosecutor and the defense counsel both realize that the prosecutor has abundant information concerning the facts of the case which, if admitted as evidence at the adjudicatory hearing, almost guarantee a finding that the allegations are true. The prosecutor wants to proceed because of this apparently "solid" case. The defense attorney denies the truth of the allegations with the hope that he can keep key pieces of the prosecutor's information from being admitted as evidence (Applicability, 1972). During these pretrial motions the admissibility of these items of information may be determined. If the judge decides that key items are not admissible as evidence, the prosecutor may logically decide to dismiss the case (figure 4, function 86) and allow the child to exit the JJS (figure 4, terminal 87). If the judge decides that the key items are admissible as evidence, the defense counsel may realistically decide that there is no hope for avoiding adjudication of delinquency. He may then advise his client to change his original denial response to admission in hopes of gaining a more favorable disposition for his belated cooperation (figure 4, function 84) (Ritter, 1968). Thus, in this example the outcome of the case is determined primarily in this prehearing motion stage (figure 4, "or" gate 85) rather than in the adjudicatory hearing (Stapleton and Teitelbaum, 1972).

If the results of preadjudicatory hearing motions and challenges do not frighten off either adversary, the process will advance to the adjudicatory hearing (figure 4, function 88). The adjudicatory hearing has two primary purposes within the context of the JJS:

1. To determine whether the child has committed the delinquent acts alleged in the petition or lesser included delinquent acts within the more serious acts alleged; and

2. If so, to determine whether the child should be adjudicated a delinquent child.

To achieve these purposes the adjudicatory hearing is essentially a factfinding hearing seeking to determine the truth of the allegations in the petition.

A date for the beginning of the adjudicatory hearing is likely to be set at the arraignment (figure 4, function 79) but may be changed after that by circumstances that arise. When the date finally arrives, the juvenile court judge will convene the adjudicatory hearing (figure 4, function 88). This step may be no more than a recording of the case number, the name of the juvenile respondent, and other administrative details of the case. Generally, the judge will merely assure himself that all is ready to begin the adjudicatory hearing. Note that juvenile hearings are very seldom before a jury, and no constitutional right to a jury exists (*McKeiver v. Pennsylvania;* Horowitz and Nickerson, 1972; Blank, 1972; Zakouro, 1972; Juvenile Courts, 1972).

The first task of the prosecutor and juvenile respondent's counsel is to make opening statements (figure 4, function 89). It is not uncommon for the prosecutor's and respondent's counsel to waive this right (Besharov, 1974: 343) and simply proceed with presentation of the evidence. However, in doing so they are waiving "the opportunity given to each side of a case to state and explain what the issues are and what the proof in support of those issues will be" (Littleton, 1966: 17). The opening statement can set the stage and provide a framework for each item of evidence to be produced.

After opening statements the prosecutor presents the evidence tending to prove the truth of the facts alleged in the petition (figure 4, function 90). The prosecutor may be the district attorney or prosecuting attorney or may be another JJS agent, typically a juvenile probation officer given this responsibility. To have this function performed by other than a skilled attorney is unadvisable. The child is represented by a competent attorney; the state should be equally well represented (Berenson, 1969). The prosecutor's task is almost identical to that in a criminal trial if the delinquent acts alleged are violations of the criminal law. That is, the case must be proved beyond a reasonable doubt (*In re Winship*). The delinquent respondent's counsel need "prove" nothing but must simply keep the prosecutor from proving the case beyond a reasonable doubt (Kay and Segal, 1973). Of course, respondent's counsel is alertly challenging the prosecutor's evidence while it is being presented. In any event, this is an adversary proceeding, and both litigants should be represented by skilled legal advocates. See recommendation 14 in chapter 5.

At the close of the prosecutor's evidence, the delinquent child's attorney will usually ask the judge to dismiss the case, claiming that the prosecutor has failed to prove it, even before any defense evidence is presented (Behsarov, 1974: 365-66). If the juvenile court decides (figure 4, "or" gate 91) that the respondent's claim is valid, the judge will dismiss the case (figure 4, function 92) and the respondent will exit the JJS (figure 4, terminal 93). Such a dismissal is rare, since such a serious lack of evidence should have convinced the prosecutor not to bring the case to court in the first place.

If the juvenile court judge decides that the prosecutor has presented a strong enough case to avoid dismissal, the child's attorney will then present evidence tending to prove that the allegations in the petition are untrue or unproven (figure 4, function 94) (Greenspan, 1969; Murphy, 1969; Weyhrich, 1968). Other defenses, such as legal insanity, are also made at this time (Popkin and Lippert, 1971). After the respondent's evidence, attorneys for both sides will make their closing rebuttals, statements, and motions (figure 4, function 95) (O'Donnell, 1972). At that point the juvenile court judge must make findings as to whether or not the facts alleged in the petition have been proved (figure 4, "or" gate 98). If the court finds that the allegations have not been sufficiently proved to amount to an act of delinquency (figure 4, function 99), the case is dismissed and the child exits the JJS (figure 4, terminal 101). If the court finds the evidence proves that the facts alleged are true or that some lesser, included act of delinquency has been proved (figure 4, function 97), the court moves on to the adjudication decision (figure 4, "or" gate 96).

If the judge adjudicates the child to be delinquent (figure 4, function 119), the case proceeds to the dispositional court subsystem (figure 4, connector 120). The other option is the last opportunity within the formal JJS to shunt the child into the informal JJS. That is, the juvenile court judge may withhold the judgment which would adjudicate delinquency (figure 4, function 100) and instead choose an informal alternative (figure 4, "or" gate 102) for the child, who has already undergone the effects of the adjudicatory hearing (Snyder, 1971). The "most informal" alternative would be for the child to be released (figure 4, function 105) and to exit the JJS (figure 4, terminal 108). This might occur if the delinquent acts had been proved but the child and family had been undergoing counseling and now seemed to have straightened out all their problems. In consistence with the goals of the JJS, the judge could avoid a formal adjudication of delinquency and the labeling problems inherent therein.

More commonly in this "last chance" diversion into the informal system, the child would either be placed on "voluntary" informal probation (figure 4, function 103) or would be referred to a social service agency for counseling (figure 4, function 104). "Voluntary," or informal, probation at this juncture is the same phenomenon described as resulting from the intake screening decision (figure 3, function 46 and thereafter). As indicated in that description, the child is required to perform in an almost identical fashion as would be required on formal probation, but no formal pronouncement of delinquency or probationary status is involved. Typically, if the child refuses to "volunteer" for informal probation, the judge adjudicates him delinquent and the formal JJS goes on from there. If the child does at the earlier stage "volunteer" for informal probation, he usually waives such basic constitutional rights as the right to counsel, right to a dispositional hearing, right to challenge evidence, etc. He is simply processed by the informal JJS in whatever manner seems appropriate, having no realistic opportunity to object or challenge decisions being made. See chapter 7 below for a further discussion of the informal JJS.

If the delinquent respondent is placed on informal probation (figure 4, function 103) and performs satisfactorily (figure 4, function 110), he will normally be "discharged" from informal probation and exit the formal JJS (figure 4, terminal 114). If he does not perform satisfactorily on informal probation (figure 4, function 109), he may still exit the JJS (figure 4, terminal 117) if it seems fruitless to have him placed in a formal correctional status. However, it could be recommended (figure 4, "or" gate 113) that the child return to the formal JJS and that the juvenile court judge enter the judgment previously withheld (figure 4, function 119).

A similar sequence occurs if the child is referred to a social service agency for counseling (figure 4, function 104). If the child responds favorably to counseling (figure 4, function 112), he exits the JJS (figure 4, terminal 116). If he responds unfavorably to counseling (figure 4, function 111), he may (figure 4, "or" gate 115) be released from the JJS (figure 4, terminal 118) or he may be sent back to the formal JJS, adjudicated delinquent (figure 4, function 119), and sent to the formal disposition subsystem (figure 4, connector 120).

The decision as to whether or not the child performed satisfactorily on informal probation or responded favorably to counseling is made ultimately by the juvenile court judge acting upon the advice and report of the probation officer or counselor. Thus, this formal or informal JJS agent has significant power over the child's future and a motivating factor to encourage compliance with informal probation or counseling. This power is largely unchecked by the court and unchallengeable by the child. Often the probation officer may resent intrusions into this functional area by the child's attorney (Brennan, 1970; Erickson, 1974). Chapter 7 discusses this situation more fully.

DISPOSITIONAL COURT SUBSYSTEM OF THE JJS

No child enters this subsystem except by being formally adjudicated delinquent by a juvenile court judge as a result of an adjudication hearing.

This subsystem is dominated by the dispositional hearing, which is the last of the three major juvenile court hearings within the JJS (waiver hearing, adjudication hearing, and disposition hearing). The purposes of the dispositional subsystem of the JJS are to determine the needs of the child and of the community, and, on the basis of that determination, order the most appropriate disposition for the child (Scarpitt and Stephenson, 1971). This JJS subsystem, perhaps more than any other JJS subsystem, is governed directly by the two masters of the JJS: the best interests of the child and the best interests of society.

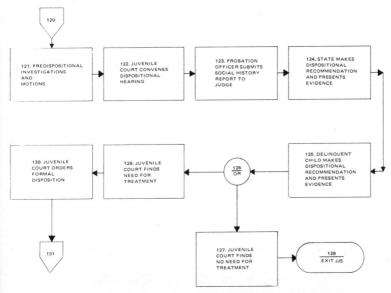

FIGURE 5. DISPOSITIONAL COURT SUBSYSTEM OF THE JJS

After the adjudication of delinquency and transfer from the adjudicatory subsystem (figure 5, connector 120), the court will schedule a disposition hearing to be preceded by pre-disposition investigations, examinations, and motions (figure 5, function 121) (Ferster and Courtless, 1972b). Of key importance is the report from pre-disposition investigation, rightfully called "the judge's most valuable guide in making a disposition" (Johnson, 1975: 117). It is typically conducted by a juvenile probation officer (Schultz, 1967; Teitelbaum, 1967). Reliance upon this social study report, while not permitted during the adjudicatory hearing (Frey and Bubany, 1972-73), is substantial during the dispositional hearing, and as a result much is expected from it:

The purpose of the social study is to give the court all available information that would be helpful in understanding the child so the court can arrive at a disposition that will have maximum effectiveness in correcting the child and protecting the community. (Johnson, 1975: 117-18)

Thus, the investigator and author of the report is asked to report all available information on how best to correct the child and protect the community (Thornberry, 1973). Such reports are commonly based on very few significant facts, and conclusions are based upon surmise and opinion. This is commonly less the fault of lack of effort and more the fault of unrealistic expectations.

Other pre-disposition examinations and motions include a psychiatric diagnosis of the child and/or family and similar information-gathering activities (Waterman, 1970). Once this information has been gathered and reports filed with the court, the juvenile court judge convenes the dispositional hearing (figure 5, function 122). As in the adjudicatory hearing, the prosecutor or probation officer will present his side of the case first. Most often the probation officer will submit the social study report to the judge (figure 5, function 123) (White, 1971) and then make a dispositional recommendation, presenting whatever evidence is deemed necessary to substantiate that recommendation (figure 5, function 124). Next the child, through his attorney, makes a dispositional recommendation and presents evidence to substantiate that recommendation (figure 5, function 125) (Walsh, 1968). In many cases the recommendations of both sides would be for the same disposition, making the choice much easier for the judge. However, it is not uncommon for the child's counsel to recommend probation or foster placement even though the probation officer recommends an institution (Equi et al., 1967). Few children eagerly seek to enter juvenile institutions. Instead, they seek to convince the judge of the appropriateness of probation in their case. Thus, the child's counsel must assist in presenting evidence favorable to a decision for probation even in the face of overwhelming evidence indicating the appropriateness of an institution. However, the efforts of the child's attorney do not necessarily result in a less harsh disposition (Duffee and Siegel, 1971).

It is at this point that the judge, in many jurisdictions, must determine if the child actually needs treatment (Pyfer, 1972). While this question may be raised at the adjudicatory hearing, the decision is almost always made at this point of the dispositional hearing (figure 5, "or" gate 126) (Besharov, 1974: 304-5). If the decision is made that the child does not need treatment (figure 5, terminal 127), the child exits the JJS (figure 5, terminal 128) (Bazelon, 1969). If the court finds that the child does need treatment (figure 5, function 129), the judge will usually order a formal disposition (figure 5, function 130) (Arthur, 1970) and the child will move on to one of the correctional subsystems of the JJS (figure 5, connector 131). Note that the final dispositional order is left to the juvenile court judge (Sherman, 1968; Chase, 1973). This "need for treatment" decision is marked by vague guidelines and unclear requirements (Gough, 1971a; Klaber, 1973). It is based upon the premise that the JJS exists to treat children, not punish them (Renn, 1973). Ergo, the JJS should not be dealing with a child that does not "need treatment." While some might conclude that the commission of serious acts of delinquency is conclusive evidence of a need for treatment, it is reasonable to suggest that some delinquent children either need no treatment because their problems have dissipated or should receive no treatment because the JJS knows of no treatment capable of dealing with the child's problems (Kittrie, 1969). This need for treatment issue remains unclear and is a developing area within juvenile law (Kapner, 1973).

COURT PROBATION SUBSYSTEM OF THE JJS

Described in the next two sections are the formal, court-ordered correctional schemes available to and commonly used by the JJS. Entry to the court probation subsystem is via the adjudicatory and dispositional hearings of the juvenile court (figure 6, connector 131). Both stages of the correctional process of the JJS (probation and institutions) serve the same two masters as other JJS subsystems: the best interests of the child and the best interests of society (Thomas, 1971). Specifically, the JJS correctional processes, both probation and institutions, are assigned the tasks of (1) preventing long-time deviant or criminal careers, (2) preventing a repetition of the child's delinquent behavior, and (3) assisting the child in achieving his potential as a productive citizen (President's Commission (2): 1967: 130–54).

In choosing a disposition (figure 6, "or" gate 135), the court has three basic alternatives available: private placement, probation, or institutionalization (Ferster and Courtless, 1972b). The court can place the child in a private, nongovernmental situation such as a military school, residential church camp, private home for boys or girls, or a private family setting, either with the child's parents or with foster parents (figure 6, function 134). If the court has evidence at a later time that the private placement has worked out satisfactorily (figure 6, function 132), the delinquent child can exit the JJS (figure 6, terminal 136). If the court

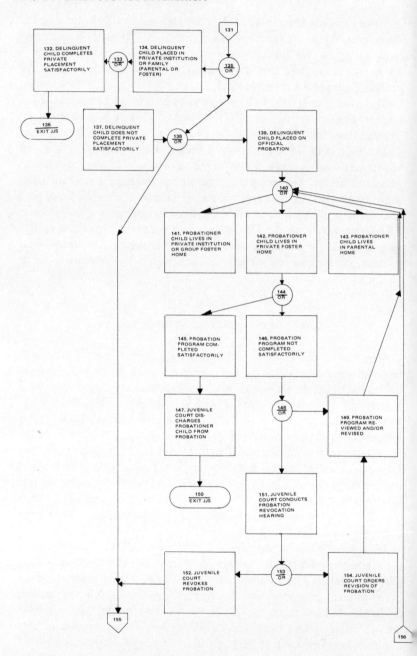

FIGURE 6. COURT PROBATION SUBSYSTEM OF THE JJS

decides (figure 6, "or" gate 133) that the private placement has not worked out satisfactorily (figure 6, function 137), the delinquent child can be returned to the mainstream of the JJS for a subsequent choice of another dispositional alternative (figure 6, "or" gate 138). Private placement such as described above is rare. Private, nonprobation alternatives available for children in trouble are almost always utilized long before this late stage in the JJS process. Indeed, placement of the misbehaving middle class youth in a private military school (out of reach financially for lower class families) is a common alternative to apprehension or formal JJS court action. It is still available as a correctional alternative in this JJS subsystem but would typically have been chosen long before now if it was a realistic alternative.

The most common dispositional decision is for the juvenile court judge to place the delinquent child on formal, official probation (figure 6, function 139) (Schwarzenberger, 1971). This dispositional alternative is designed to achieve the goals of the juvenile correctional process by supervision and counseling of the delinquent child and his family while permitting the child to remain at large within the community (Loftquist, 1967; McHardy, 1973). When placed on probation, a somewhat structured program is created for the probationer child which involves a decision about where he will live while on probation (figure 6, "or" gate 140). Familiar alternatives include a private institution or group foster home (figure 6, function 141) (James, 1971), a private foster home with a typical nuclear family (figure 6, function 142), or the probationer child's own parental home (figure 6, function 143) (Garabedian and Gibbons, 1971). First choice would normally be the child's own parental home with a private institution or group foster home as a last resort.

Of course, the probation treatment program usually includes much more than a place to live. The three major elements of effective probationary supervision and treatment are surveillance, service, and counseling (President's Commission (2), 1967: 132). The probation officer's surveillance of the probationer child keeps the officer informed as to the degree to which the requirements of probation are being met and provides an opportunity for constant assistance and guidance for the probationer child in the myriad of social situations in which he must function (Fant, 1969; Sheridan, 1968). The probation officer provides service to the probationer child by matching his needs with community service agencies equipped to serve such needs. The counseling aspect of probation requires the officer to interact with the child on a person-to-person basis in order to achieve the first two aspects of probation. While on probation, the child retains many rights, including the services of an attorney if he wishes (Lockwood, 1968).

Whether or not a probationer completes probation satisfactorily (figure 6, "or" gate 144) depends as much upon the services made available by the probation officer and community service agencies as it does upon the desire and ability of the probationer child to succeed. If the probation program is completed satisfactorily (figure 6, function 145), the probationer child will be released from probation (figure 6, function 147) and will exit the JJS (figure 6, terminal 150). If it is not completed satisfactorily by the probationer child (figure 6, function 146), the probation officer decides what to do about it (figure 6, "or" gate 148). The probation officer may decide to review and/or revise the child's probation treatment program (figure 6, function 149) and then begin again in a new probation mode (figure 6, "or" gate 140). The probation officer may decide to recommend revocation of probation and cause the juvenile court to conduct a probation revocation hearing (figure 6, function 151) complete with evidence and the probationer's attorney (Ismael, 1972). As a result of that hearing (figure 6, "or" gate 153), the juvenile court may opt for continued probation and order revision of the probation program (figure 6, function 154), resulting in continued probation in the new mode. If the juvenile court judge decides to revoke probation (figure 6, function 152), the child moves on to the institution subsystem of the JJS (figure 6, connector 155).

Discontinuance of probation could also come from another judicial sentencing technique. At the original disposition hearing (see figure 5) the juvenile court judge could order (figure 5, function 130) institutionalization, suspend that order, and place the delinquent child on probation (figure 6, function 139). If probation is not completed satisfactorily, the institutionalization order can be "unsuspended" and the delinquent child will move on to the institution subsystem of the JJS (figure 6, connector 155).

INSTITUTION SUBSYSTEM OF THE JJS

This JJS subsystem fittingly comes at the end of this JJS description. This subsystem processes very few children compared to the previous JJS subsystems. State-operated institutions for delinquent children are the last resort of the correctional subsystem (McCarty, 1973), to be utilized only if the child is too unstable or hardened to be appropriate for a less restrictive dispositional alternative (President's Commission, 1967 (2): 141; Culbertson, 1973). This dispositional alternative tends to provide the most physical protection for the general public during the delinquent child's correctional program but in the end may convert a delinquent child into an adult criminal who will be a very serious threat to the general public when released (Cole, 1972; Simms, 1972). In too many cases our society trades avoidance of annoying delinquent acts now for the guarantee of serious criminal acts in a few years from now (Rogers, 1972). However, for the child who has committed and gives every indication of continuing to commit serious antisocial acts, particularly involving violence against the person, the juvenile institution is apparently the only appropriate dispositional choice now available (Pirsig, 1969).

Even after the judge has committed the delinquent child to a state juvenile institution (figure 7, function 157), some jurisdictions permit the judge to decide (figure 7, "or" gate 158) within a few weeks or months to consider the child for a "shock probation" program (figure 7, function 159). Under such a program the child is removed from the institution after having received a clear impression of what incarceration for a longer period would be like. Theoretically, this technique provides a specific deterrent for that child to avoid future delinquent behavior and avoid ending up in the state institution with no hope of early release through shock probation. If the judge decides (figure 7, "or" gate 160) to grant shock probation (figure 7, function 161), the delinquent child is thereafter handled as other delinquent probationers (figure 7, connector 156). If the judge decides to deny shock probation (figure 7, function 163), the delinquent child returns to the normal institutional sequence (Hynes, 1972). At this point the institution places the delinquent child on a treatment program (figure 7, function 162) (Fox, 1972: 308-15; Chase, 1974) administered primarily by the institution but subject to judicial overview (Clark, 1972; Cooley, 1971; Fairlie, 1972).

Once on the institutional treatment program, the delinquent child is generally not released until the maximum age limit is reached (figure 7, "or" gate 164), the maximum time of the disposition is served (figure 7, "or" gate 169), or he "satisfies the treatment program" at the institution (figure 7, "or" gate 175) (Bottoms and McClintock, 1974; Clemens, 1969). If he reaches the maximum age limit for the institution (figure 7, function 165), the institution must release the child (figure 7, function 166), and he exits the JJS (figure 7, terminal 168). If the child remains under the maximum age limit for the institution (figure 7, function 167) but has served the maximum time of the disposition (figure 7, function 170), the institution releases the child (figure 7, function 171) and he exits the JJS (figure 7, terminal 173). If the child has not served the maximum time of the disposition (figure 7, function 172), he moves to the decision about his performance on the institution's program (figure 7, "or" gate 175). The release points above do not necessarily occur before or after the other release points. This analytical method is presented simply to

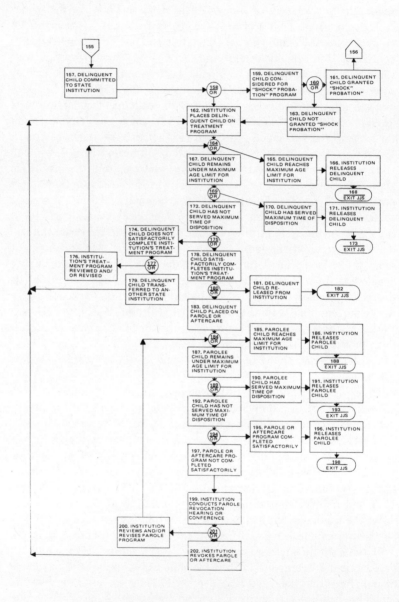

FIGURE 7. INSTITUTION SUBSYSTEM OF THE JJS

illustrate that the child must be released by the institution if the maximum time limit is reached, regardless of the child's performance in the institution's treatment program. This is a fixed requirement which may tend to make achievement of treatments goals somewhat irrelevant.

Institutions make periodic reviews of each child's progress to see if the child might have reached a proper point for release or parole from the institution (figure 7, "or" gate 175) (Juvenile, 1967). If the determination is made that the delinquent has not satisfactorily completed the institution's treatment program (figure 7, function 174), the institutional staff may decide (figure 7, "or" gate 177) to revise the treatment program or/and to review with the child his progress (figure 7, function 176) (Scott and Hissong, 1969). The child remains within that institutional scheme. However, in some cases the institutional staff may decide to transfer the child to another state institution (figure 7, function 179), particularly when the child is uncontrollable and dangerous within the setting of the original institution (Hausman, 1972; Facts, 1968).

If the institutional staff decides (figure 7, "or" gate 175) that the delinquent has satisfactorily completed the institution's treatment program (figure 7, function 178), at least to a point where a closed setting is no longer needed, they may decide (figure 7, "or" gate 180) to release the child completely from the institution (figure 7, function 181), and thus the child exits the JJS (figure 7, terminal 182). More commonly the delinquent child will be placed on juvenile parole, often euphemistically referred to as "aftercare" (figure 7, function 183) (Arnold, 1970).

Similarly, if the child on aftercare reaches the maximum age limit for the institution (figure 7, function 185) or has served the maximum time of the disposition (figure 7, function 190), the institution parole or aftercare officer must release the juvenile parolee (figure 7, functions 186 and 191, respectively), and the child exits the JJS (figure 7, terminals 188 and 193, respectively). If the juvenile parolee remains under the maximum age limit for the institution (figure 7, function 187) and has not served the maximum time of the disposition (figure 7, function 192), the decision is made concerning his performance on the aftercare program (figure 7, "or" gate 194) (Hussey, 1976). If the institution and aftercare officers decide that the aftercare program has been completed satisfactorily (figure 7, function 195), they will release the child (figure 7, function 196), and he will exit the JJS (figure 7, terminal 198).

If the institution and aftercare officers decide that the aftercare program has not been satisfactorily completed (figure 7, function 197), they will conduct a parole/aftercare revocation hearing or conference (figure 7, function 199) to decide what to do with the juvenile parolee (figure 7, "or" gate 201) (Sarosiek, 1973). They may decide to revise the aftercare program and/or review the program with the child (figure 7, function 200) and then continue the child on aftercare. However, they may decide to revoke the child's parole or aftercare (figure 7, function 202) and take the child back into the institution.

Thus, the correctional subsystems of the JJS are completed. If all has gone according to theory, the child who entered as a formally labeled juvenile delinquent exits a rehabilitated young person, ready, willing, and able to pursue a productive, law-abiding life.

4. JJS PHILOSOPHY AND DESIGN

PROBLEMS AND RECOMMENDATIONS

The foregoing history and functional description of the JJS revealed several dilemmas, several clashes between JJS goals and agency practices, and several issues deserving of further discussion. The next four chapters will deal with those points and suggest insights from which some recommendations may be made. The discussions will be primarily in the form of arguments for one recommendation or conclusion. These arguments are presented in a manner intended to stimulate debate and further thinking about the issues involved.

From the beginning the JJS has been fundamentally different from the criminal justice system in at least one respect. The criminal justice system broadly proclaims and meticulously tries to protect a fundamental right to liberty, including the right not to be arrested or interfered with except for very good reason, the right not to be incarcerated or restrained unless absolutely necessary, and the right to do generally as we please as long as we stay within very broad limits. Conversely, the JJS is founded on a fundamental right to proper parental custody, such custody to be provided by the governmental parent if for some reason it is not being provided by the natural parents. Thus, while adults have a fundamental legal right to be free of governmental intervention in their life except in certain circumstances, children have a fundamental right to receive governmental intervention in their life unless they are being properly cared for by their natural parents (Streib, 1973).

The background of this fundamental right to proper parental custody is pervasive, and this right seems not likely to disappear in the foreseeable future. However, this JJS right to custody clashes directly with the emerging childrens' rights movement and specifically with the constitutional rights to Fourteenth Amendment due process afforded delinquent respondents by *Gault* and its progeny. The clash between constitutional due process and the traditional right to custody is the philosophical undercurrent of misunderstandings and differences of opinion between delinquent respondents' attorneys and probation officers (Brennan, 1970). The probation officer may see his or her responsibility within the JJS as facilitating and implementing the governmental parenting for which the JJS was established and which the child so clearly needs (Loftquist, 1967). The delinquent respondent's attorney may see his or her responsibility within the JJS as insuring that the child's constitutional rights are protected and that the JJS is not permitted to impose any sanctions or other inconveniences upon the child unless authorized by law (Kay and Segal, 1973). If both these JJS professionals believed in a right to proper parental custody, both would work toward provision of that parental custody as quickly and efficiently as possible. However, the law does not permit the delinquent respondent's attorney to act in such a manner but rather requires the attorney to resist this governmental intervention on behalf of the child, assuming the child desires such resistance.

The child caught up in the JJS typically will have a strong opinion about his need for proper parental custody and/or his desire for governmental parenting. It is most rare for a delinquent child to seek restrictive custody from natural parents or from a governmental substitute. While children may seek adequate room and board, few children seek these necessities at the local jail or the state juvenile institution. The JJS right to custody is not generally understood or exerted by the children being served by the JJS and for whom this fundamental right was created. The JJS right to custody was based upon hope and aspiration never achieved in practice. Implementation of this "impossible dream" has resulted in a mockery of our society's conception of proper parental care.

RECOMMENDATION 1: THE JJS SHOULD REPUDIATE THE "RIGHT TO CUSTODY" PREMISE FOR ALLEGED DELINQUENTS UNTIL GOVERNMENTAL CUSTODY CAN AND DOES APPROXIMATE PROPER PARENTAL CARE.

As has been said repeatedly, the "two masters" of the JJS are the best interests of the child and the best interests of society. A basic JJS philosophical problem is the bastardization of these two guiding principles into two divergent battlecries of various JJS agents and concerned commentators. One battlecry is based on the best interests of society and seeks to use the JJS to control juvenile crime, particularly in its more violent and costly manifestations. The notion of "getting tough on crime" affects juvenile crime as well as adult crime and thus becomes a primary operating principle for many JJS agents. The best interests of society are defined as maximum protection from the present threat of crime.

Other JJS agents follow the guiding philosophy of the best interests of the child and interpret this as meaning help for the child in an appropriate form. The alternatives of prehearing detention or incarceration in an institution are to be avoided at almost all costs since they do not help the child but rather make the child's problems even worse. If the battlecry is to help the child, then any actions which tend to harm the child are to be avoided strenuously.

This clash between battlecries or operating principles is most apparent at the dispositional hearing when the judge is considering institutionalization of the child. The child's previous violent, antisocial acts and lack of apparent resolution to discontinue such acts understandably leads the judge to consider institutionalization as the only means of controlling such violence or at least restricting it to inside the walls of a juvenile institution. Following the operating principle of "getting tough on crime" and protecting the peace and order of society, institutionalization seems the only rational dispositional choice.

However, the opposite faction would argue against institutionalization, since institutionalization of the child will almost certainly harm the child's personality, self-conception, opportunity for personal growth, probability of avoiding adult criminal acts, etc. Moreover, the child's violent, antisocial tendencies will not be prevented. The locale of the violent acts will be within the institution and the victims of the violent acts will be other children or staff within the institution (Wenk and Emrich, 1972). Of course, the child will also be the victim of violent acts by others in the institution, besides being indoctrinated in ways of criminal life never available to him at home.

This corruption and bastardization of the two masters of the JJS reveal shallow thinking and antihumanistic motivations. The JJS should continue to serve both the best interests of the child and the best interests of society, but need not go to extremes in either direction. Being "tough on crime" by increasing the length, frequency, and harshness of juvenile dispositions serves neither interest. This battlecry suggests a basic hatred for all deviants, particularly deviant children, and should not be allowed rational consideration within the JJS. Not as disgusting but nevertheless a problem is the tendency to help the child regardless of societal cost. This also does not serve the child or society, since contemporary knowledge provides scant information on how to help the child effectively.

Moreover, all this profferred "help" presents a very unrealistic picture of society to the child who must live the rest of his life in a remarkably uncaring, apathetic world in which self-reliance is essential to survival. Given these parameters, the JJS should return to a balance of the two philosophical masters and avoid extremism in implementation of either philosophy.

RECOMMENDATION 2: THE JJS SHOULD SERVE THE BEST INTERESTS OF THE CHILD AND THE BEST INTERESTS OF SOCIETY IN EQUAL MEASURE AND AVOID SACRIFICE OF ONE OR THE OTHER FOR EXPEDIENCE.

A third JJS problem, partly of philosophy but mostly of design, is the clash between Anglo-American law's demand for *procedure* and Anglo-American social service's demand for *results*. The attitude of law was made clear in *Gault* by the United States Supreme Court's clear and un-equivocal demand for proper legal procedure within the JJS. Indeed, the constitutionalization of the JJS through application of the provisions of Fourteenth Amendment due process could more revealingly be labeled the "proceduralization" of the JJS. As long as the JJS is a legal system dominated by a legal court, proper legal procedure will be demanded.

JSS agents and agencies which see themselves primarily as "people-helpers" may understandably have less concern for procedure than for meaningful results. They believe that even if the JJS operates very ef-ficiently and all functions are performed precisely as required, it may still be meaningless if the children being served receive nothing of value from the system/servant. Such JJS agents look first to the value of the services being provided to the children and then try to fit the service-providing activities within the general requirements of the law. For example, if the JJS agent perceives that the child "obviously needs" professional counseling but due process of law makes imposition of such counseling difficult if not impossible, then the child may be coerced into "volunteering" for unofficial, informal probation so that the needed services can be delivered. In this manner the procedural requirements are followed only as long as they don't hinder the achievement of the desired result (as perceived by the JJS agent), and means are devised to circumvent the procedural requirements whenever necessary.

This clash between procedure and results will be largely unavoidable as long as the JJS is partly a legal system and partly a social welfare system. However, proponents of either objective should be educated in the reasons behind the strong desires for each objective (Fant, 1969). The primary problem lies with the proponents of results regardless of procedural requirements. Such proponents must be educated in the basic Anglo-American legal principle of "rule of law, not of men" and the understandable desire of our society to avoid despotism, regardless of whether it is centered in the White House, the court, or the probation office. For many reasons firmly rooted in the experiences of the human race, despots claiming benevolence as their sole motivation are to be avoided. Procedural rules equally applicable to all cases are a primary means we have found to avoid such calamities, and such procedural rules need not prevent the achievement of desired results.

RECOMMENDATION 3: THE JJS SHOULD STRENGTHEN AND INCREASE ITS PROCEDURAL REQUIREMENTS FOR DELINQUENCY CASES AND EDUCATE ALL JJS AGENTS AS TO THE REASONS FOR AND USE OF THESE PROCEDURAL REQUIREMENTS.

A fourth JJS design problem is that we have designed a sociolegal system to administer and deliver an entity not yet in existence. JJS rhetoric concerning the "treatment of delinquency" seems to assume that such "treatment" is within human knowledge and capabilities. While the number of theories on the treatment of delinquency seems to match or exceed the number of theorists, the enormous disagreement among the theorists plus the paucity of credible evidence that the treatment modes have meaningful effects inescapably lead us to but one conclusion. This area of human knowledge is still in an embryonic stage; not only do we not have many answers but we are not even certain of the proper questions.

Examples of this lack of knowledge are varied and numerous. Consider the group foster home which enthusiastically tells of its subtle behavior modification program humanistically administered in a nuclear family setting. If few of the delinquent residents are subsequently arrested for criminal acts, the group foster home claims a very high success rate. However, careful analysis reveals that the home has a very restrictive admissions screening program which admits only very low risk delinquents who show every sign of maturing out of the delinquent behavior by themselves regardless of treatment. Also, the very low probability of arrest for a criminal act leads one to question the home's claim of no subsequent delinquency proven by no subsequent arrests. Moreover, the home's political motivation to cover up any subsequent delinquent acts further muddles the picture. Those that claim this mode of treatment is effective in reducing delinquency have an argument that most of us would like to believe because of our strong faith in the institution of the nuclear family. However, close inspection reveals little or no basis for that belief.

Consider the delinquency "treatment" mode of the threat of lengthy, restrictive incarceration in a juvenile institution in order to scare children into avoiding delinquent acts. If the delinquency rate goes up or down, can we in any manner assume this was caused by the threat of a harsh disposition? Given the very low adjudication/conviction rate for all cases of burglary, robbery, rape, and many other serious delinquent acts which are violations of criminal laws, the unlikely possibility of receiving an admittedly harsh disposition is a questionable deterrent. If a child is subjected to institutionalization for a long period of time, and, after release, is not subsequently arrested for criminal offenses, can we conclude that the person has been rehabilitated or, if so, that institutionalization was the cause of the rehabilitation?

It seems clear that each person promoting one treatment mode or another does so primarily out of faith, hope, and perhaps a desire to stay employed or increase his empire of funds and employees. Most students of the treatment of delinquency can make a plausible argument for any treatment mode. Few are willing to admit the very thin factual basis for such arguments.

RECOMMENDATION 4: THE JJS SHOULD OPENLY ADMIT ITS VERY THIN KNOWLEDGE BASE AND PERMIT ONLY THOSE TREATMENT MODES NECESSARY FOR PROTECTION OF SOCIETY OR TO BE TRIED ON A SMALL-SCALE, CAREFULLY MONITORED EXPERIMENTAL BASIS.

An obvious flaw in the design of the JJS is the lack of a system manager and the apathy of poorly informed system designers (Law, 1971). The very nature of the JJS as an Anglo-American legal system makes it impossible for it to have a true system manager such as one might find in a manufacturing production system, a management information system, or a home heating system. Several JJS agents, notably the juvenile court judge and the juvenile probation officer, have tried to "coordinate" or facilitate cooperation within the JJS. However, neither of these attempts has had much beneficial effect. The juvenile court judge has substantial power within the JJS but seldom has the interest, knowledge, or political motivation to act as a system manager. The United States Supreme Court followed a "hands off" policy toward the JJS for the entire socialized era and stepped in only when it could no longer ignore the adverse effects that the out-of-control system was having upon children.

Attempts by juvenile probation officers to coordinate or manage JJS agents and agencies, while not so commonly defeated by lack of interest or of knowledge, more often fail because of lack of power to require JJS agents and agencies to consider seriously their recommendations. The juvenile probation officer functions at more junctures within the JJS than any other JJS agent except the juvenile's attorney. The juvenile probation officer works with the police at the detention and intake stages, with the prosecutor and judge at the hearing stages, and with the treatment agencies at the dispositional stages. However, the juvenile probation officer does not enjoy the community and JJS respect accorded to a judge and in many cases has been characterized as a political hack rewarded by the local machine for faithful allegiance to the political party. This image is changing in many communities, but current efforts at change will be some time in achieving the goals.

No other JJS agent seems appropriate to assume leadership within the JJS. The child's attorney has a far-ranging role in which many agents and agencies are contacted and negotiated with, but the nature of the role as "defense attorney" fatally limits the attorney in forcing any meaningful compliance with system management suggestions or decrees. The police officers involved in juvenile work have a relatively limited scope of operation and do not seem to be able to command the respect that a system manager would need. Juvenile institutions are likewise isolated from the mainstream of the JJS and have minimal contact with other JJS agents and agencies.

Only one possibility remains, and that is the primary system designer: the legislature. The legislature is the primary designer of the JJS in that it establishes the acts of delinquency, defines the jurisdiction of the juvenile courts, determines when juveniles may be apprehended and detained, and establishes basic guidelines for juvenile institutions. Since the JJS is a legal system, it is established by law and changes in its design are made through law. Of course, the courts also establish and modify laws which govern the JJS but not as comprehensively and without the legislature's ability to consider the overall system in doing so.

Changes in fundamental JJS philosophy and design can and should be made by legislative bodies. The legislature has the unique ability and responsibility to examine the entire JJS as a system and to institute changes with a consideration for systemic effects. The legislatures are the only entities capable of being both the system designer/redesigner and the system manager. System management by the legislature can be accomplished by statutes requiring certain agencies to perform certain tasks and functions and by exercising budgetary control over the agencies and agents. Admittedly, such system design and management is from afar and fraught with administrative difficulties, but thus far the JJS has limped along with very poor system design and almost no system management. Legislative efforts would be a step in the right direction.

RECOMMENDATION 5: THE JJS SHOULD ENLIST THE APPROPRIATE LEGISLATIVE BODY TO REVISE THE JJS DESIGN AND TO ACT AS THE SYSTEM MANAGER.

One final observation must be made concerning JJS philosophy. The JJS, as with all Anglo-American legal systems, by implication teaches that obeying the laws is good, intelligent, and profitable while violating the laws is bad, stupid, and costly. If our children were as naive and uninformed as many of us apparently assume, such teaching might be appropriate and might even result in a large percentage of children who believe such teachings to be true. However, our children are perceptive observers of the real world as it compares to the teachings of the JJS. Our children know as well as we do that almost all of us are law violators and a person's legal problems come not from violating the law but from being caught without an adequate defense after violating the law. Since American rhetoric constantly reminds us that we are basically a good people and since it is apparent that we are also a law-violating people, our children rightly question the assertion that good people don't violate laws and that law violators are bad people. For example, children may look to their parents, teachers, television heroes, and national leaders as examples of good people. They realize quite clearly that their parents violate laws (e.g., speed on the highway and cheat on income tax), their teachers violate laws (e.g., conduct illegal strikes and gamble on the outcome of a ballgame), television heroes violate laws (e.g., commit assault and battery against the bad guys), and national leaders violate laws (e.g., Watergate). To continue claiming that good people don't violate laws is to appear as fools in the eyes of our children.

Our children also realize that it is not always intelligent to obey the law or stupid to violate the laws. When they see their friends shoplift regularly to get items that they are doing without, the stupid person seems to be the law obeyer and not the law violator. To claim repeatedly that it is profitable to obey the law and costly to violate the law is also to ignore reality. Our children, particularly those we have consigned to our urban and rural ghettos, clearly understand the illegality of the occupation of the pimp or prostitute wearing the expensive clothes and driving the expensive automobile. They also understand the legality of the occupation of the janitor or laborer and the relative unprofitability of such endeavors. Until our society is capable of making legal occupations more profitable than illegal occupations, to claim that the opposite situation obtains is to make the JJS appear to be totally ignorant of reality (Crime's, 1976). Moreover, to claim that the cost of law violation is the juvenile disposition administered after adjudication is to ignore facts our children know well—the JJS rarely adjudicates delinquent law violators and even more rarely imposes a harsh disposition.

Wish as we might, we cannot justify presenting the world as it is not, never has been, and may never be in the future. This refusal of adults to admit what our children clearly understand may be a major cause of the "generation gap." We told our children that engaging in sex or drug use would have horrifying effects upon them. When they did so engage and found our claims to be wholly without foundation in fact, the loss in credibility was immeasurable. When we tell our children that the world is one way while all their evidence indicates the opposite, we cannot realistically expect much subsequent respect for what we say.

The JJS should not provide one more vehicle for hypocrisy. The JJS should unequivocally admit that almost all children commit acts of delinquency while growing up and almost all adults commit criminal acts. Because of screening systems which have arisen in society and the JJS, certain children are selected to receive a reaction from the JJS because of being caught committing an act of delinquency. While it is not particularly good to commit acts of delinquency, most so-called good kids do commit such acts. Further, it is not "stupid" to commit acts of delinquency, because admittedly many intelligent people do so; and admittedly it is unlikely that one would be caught if he did commit an act of delinquency. Moreover, the available evidence indicates quite clearly that crime does pay (Crime's, 1976) and that the most "profitable" activities for poorly educated and unacculturated minority young persons in urban ghettos are such activities as prostitution, illegal drug sales, and illegal gambling. While it is admittedly a sad commentary on our society, to claim otherwise will not magically change society into our dream world but will only destroy any credibility that JJS agencies have with our children.

RECOMMENDATION 6: THE JJS SHOULD OPENLY ADMIT THE PERVASIVENESS OF JUVENILE DELINQUENCY IN OUR SOCIETY, THE IRRATIONALITY OF THE PROCESSES BY WHICH CHILDREN ARE CHOSEN FOR TREATMENT BY THE JJS, AND THE LACK OF JUSTIFICATION, OTHER THAN PERSONAL VALUE SYSTEMS, FOR OBEYING MOST CRIMINAL AND JUVENILE LAWS.

5. JJS OPERATIONS

PROBLEMS AND RECOMMENDATIONS

In addition to problems and issues in JJS philosophy and design, there are important problems and issues having more to do with the actions and activities of juvenile justice agencies. These involve day-to-day realities of operating the JJS and reacting to real, nonacademic problems and issues that arise. Moreover, the recommendations in this area are more pragmatic and, as a result, more easily implemented.

POLICE OPERATIONAL PROBLEMS AND RECOMMENDATIONS

Let us begin with the police functions within the JJS. A primary police activity—apprehension of the suspected delinquent—almost always has a partially self-defeating effect. A major goal of the JJS is to rehabilitate the delinquent child, but the original apprehension tends to label the child, for his own perspective and for the perspective of his peer group, parents, neighbors, and teachers (Schur, 1971). That is, regardless of the rhetoric about "innocent until proven guilty," we know that police typically do not apprehend children unless they have substantial evidence ("probable cause") to believe the child has committed an act of delinquency. Regardless of the fiction writers' popular theme of the innocent child persecuted by agents of the law, almost all children apprehended by the police are guilty of the act alleged or something quite like the act alleged. Therefore, if a child is apprehended by the police we tend to form a barely rebuttable presumption of delinquency. And, if he is later released or dismissed by the juvenile court, we may assume not that the child was innocent but that the state could not prove guilt or that a clever lawyer "got him off."

The apprehension stage draws the child into the JJS, from which it is most difficult to extricate himself. Even if the child escapes through one of the many exit JJS terminals, the community does not allow absolute escape. The child is branded as a potential delinquent or "predelinquent" by the community and by JJS agents, greatly increasing the probability of apprehension and processing by the JJS for subsequent delinquent acts. Much like the fabled bulldog, the JJS is hard to shake once it gets its teeth into a child.

Police apprehension of juveniles is an unncessary, expensive, and irreparably damaging JJS activity in many delinquency cases (Schur, 1971). In the vast majority of cases, a simple court summons can be issued by the juvenile court to the child and his parents or guardians and police apprehension can be avoided completely (Fox, 1971: 83-99). The summons process can be kept confidential and avoids the spectacular "cowboyism" of police apprehension. The summons process also avoids the degrading and highly punitive ride to the police station in the back of a squad car and the juvenile booking procedures at the police station. It is clear that JJS punishment begins partly at the investigatory stage and pervasively at the apprehension stage (Gold and Williams, 1969). To be abruptly removed from your home or neighborhood and taken into custody, transported to the police station as a criminal would be, and subjected to the dehumanizing booking process are punishments which should be limited to only those cases in which apprehension and immediate detention are essential to protect the community against acts of violence (Schur, 1973). In cases involving delinquent acts other than acts of violence, the summons procedure is just as effective, much less expensive, and avoids many of the damaging side effects of apprehension.

RECOMMENDATION 7: THE JJS POLICE SHOULD NOT AP-
PREHEND ANY DELINQUENT SUSPECT UNLESS EVIDENCE
INDICATES THAT THE SUSPECT WILL COMMIT FUTURE
ACTS OF VIOLENCE IF NOT APPREHENDED AND PHYSI-
CALLY DETAINED.

Another police action problem or issue is the postapprehension/pre-hearing detention of alleged delinquent children. As argued above concerning apprehension, detention of juveniles is defensible only for those children who pose an actual threat of violence to the community if they are allowed to be free. Detention of alleged delinquents may render subsequent treatment much more unlikely to succeed (Mora, 1969).

The JJS in most jurisdictions does not have juvenile detention centers separate or different from adult detention centers. Although laws typically require that children not be incarcerated directly with adults, this requirement is often satsified by designating a separate section or floor of the county jail as the "juvenile detention center." Some jurisdictions even go so far as to have a separate entrance for juveniles. However, our children clearly perceive what we refuse to admit. This is a jail.

If apprehending suspected delinquents tends to label them as delinquent and thus give them a set of standards by which to conduct themselves, detention of these children most certainly does so (Brusten, 1972). Children, even more than adults, are strongly influenced by their peer groups and fellow travelers. Children in jail (or "detention centers") do not include a wide variety of children from all backgrounds or with all value systems. Children in jail are typically selected from that group of children for whom serious antisocial acts are common and who are quite sophisticated in their delinquent lifestyle. If we choose to place a child in such an environment, we are denying him access to any peer group pressure except that of the worst kind. We must admit, to ourselves even if not to the child, that such detention indicates we consider his case almost hopeless and thus are not particularly concerned if our terminally ill patient contracts yet more terminal illnesses.

Consider the many deprivations visited upon the child by prehearing detention. If the child is enrolled in school, classes are missed and he falls behind in school work. A large percentage of delinquent children are having difficulty in school, and adding to these difficulties does not seem wise. If the child works part-time, he misses work and quite likely will lose his job. A strong argument can be made for the beneficial effects of a job for delinquent children, so it seems counterproductive for the JJS to contribute to their losing their jobs (Kobetz and Bosarge, 1973).

JJS agents too commonly believe that prehearing detention will provide the same effect as shock probation, in that a relatively brief time in punitive incarceration will bring the child to his senses and apprise him of the results of criminal activity. Some apparently believe that a few days or weeks in jail will provide much needed time for the child to think, and to gain respect for the law. This assumption has no basis in research data and seems to ignore obvious points. Our county jails are the worst examples of incarceration units, are generally in the worst state of repair, offer the fewest services to children, and have the fewest facilities for inmates. To believe that such an institution will instill respect in a child for the majesty of law is foolish. It is equally foolish to believe that a child in such a depressing, hostile, antihuman environment, devoid of counselors, parents, friends, or any manifestations of normal society, would resolve to begin acting less hostile, more human, and relate to normal society in a more acceptable manner.

Postapprehension/prehearing detention of juveniles should be avoided unless absolutely necessary. If recommendation 6 is followed and apprehension of juveniles is limited to only those who show clear tendencies to commit future acts of violence, then detention will regularly follow apprehension of such latter children. However, if a child is apprehended who does not demonstrate such violent propensities, he should not be detained pending further proceedings. Moreover, the policy of prehearing detention for shock punitive purposes is clearly in direct opposition to JJS goals, objectives, and operating principles.

RECOMMENDATION 8: THE JJS SHOULD NOT PERMIT POST-APPREHENSION/PREHEARING DETENTION OF DELINQUENT SUSPECTS UNLESS EVIDENCE INDICATES THAT THE SUSPECT WILL COMMIT FUTURE ACTS OF VIOLENCE IF NOT DETAINED.

The next problem or issue concerning JJS actions is the point at which police, individually or collectively, consider whether or not to refer a suspected delinquency case to juvenile court. This is an area of vast, almost unchecked police discretion which can and does have a significant impact on the functioning and effectiveness of the JJS. If police select only a few delinquent children representing only a few groups within society, the JJS is denied a substantial opportunity for impact upon other delinquent children representing other groups within our society. The police may function as the primary screening agent, determining in effect which children need JJS treatment and which children do not need such treatment. This decision, fraught with incomplete diagnoses, inaccurate information, and biased assumptions, is very difficult for even the most highly trained professionals to make. For such a critical decision to be made by police officers is a highly questionable practice.

We cannot ignore the fact that the further into the JJS the child is drawn, the more intrusive, disruptive, and punitive the JJS is for the child. If the individual officer decides to end the case with nothing more than a stern lecture and a report to the parents of the child's actions, the JJS has allowed minimal intrusion into and disruption of the lives of the child, parents, and friends. If the JJS progresses further in such a case—apprehension, booking, detention, etc.—the punitive dimension of the system increases greatly and may well not be justifiable in a given case. Thus, there are good reasons for police decisions not to intervene substantially in a case.

The reasons that police discretion should intervene are far outweighed by the reasons against permitting such police discretion. Practice reveals that police tend to discriminate quite directly against certain minority groups and tend to present an entirely different concept of juvenile justice to more favored groups in our society (Ferdinand and Luchterband, 1970). This racial, cultural, and economic discrimination is apparently unavoidable as long as we lodge such vast discretion in police officers who are recruited from segments of our society in which such racial, cultural, and economic bias is commonplace. Moreover, such discretion is clearly in conflict with our premise of "rule of law, not of men."

It is not being suggested that police officers should take into custody all juvenile offenders they encounter. That is the opposite of what was suggested in recommendation 7 above. What is being suggested is an almost mechanical, routine referral to subsequent stages in the JJS of almost all cases coming to the attention of police. Police officers, either individually or as an agency, do not have the training or occupational perspective to exercise appropriate discretion in screening children out of the JJS. Police officers should investigate all reported offenses, apprehend dangerous juveniles when necessary, and report uncovered facts to the juvenile court in a routine, nonjudgmental manner. A police officer should not be permitted to act as investigator, screening officer, prosecutor, defense attorney, judge, and treatment officer all in one person; that is impossible for the most highly trained, most objective person imaginable. Police officers should be restricted to a quite limited role within the JJS. If certain cases are to be screened out and not processed further by the JJS, this decision should be made by a professional screening officer and not by a police officer.

RECOMMENDATION 9: THE JJS SHOULD REQUIRE THAT POLICE OFFICERS REPORT INFORMATION THEY HAVE CONCERNING ALMOST ALL ACTS OF DELINQUENCY AND ALMOST ALL SUSPECTED DELINQUENTS, AND SCREEN OUT ALMOST NO CASES FROM FURTHER ATTENTION BY THE JJS.

A closely related problem or issue is police involvement with children who commit noncriminal but delinquent status offenses such as running away, truancy, and incorrigibility. While a strong argument can be made for eliminating entirely such offenses from the JJS, even if they remain a part of the JJS the police should not be involved. Police reaction to criminal offenses committed by adults or children is acceptable since no adequate substitute for such police reaction is available. However, to allot the very scarce resource of police time and effort to juvenile status offenses is to make unavailable such time and effort for reaction to violent criminal acts. It is counterproductive to treat the misbehaving child as a criminal, complete with investigation, apprehension, booking, and jail. It is just such processing which will introduce the misbehaving child to children and adults involved in criminal behavior.

Police action should be restricted to those children who commit acts which would be crimes if committed by adults. Children who commit other acts of delinquency, disruptive but not criminal, should not be subject to police investigation, apprehension, or custody in any form. Such acts should be investigated by probation officers, school counselors, special truancy officers, agencies concerned with runaway children, family welfare workers, and other nonpolice JJS and JJS-related agencies. The truant child is a subject of concern for parents and school officials, not for police. The incorrigible child is a subject of concern for parents and family counselors, not for police. Such children should have the right to be free of police intervention in their lives even though they have violated a delinquency law which is based upon strong societal and cultural beliefs and mores. As was suggested in recommendation 1, the "right to proper parental custody" should not be used to justify handling such children as if they were criminals. While such behavior is arguably of legitimate concern to society and to the JJS, the police function should be circumvented entirely.

If police were prevented from dealing with such children, other agencies would have to be created or strengthened to cope with them. Young children who run away from their small-town home to experience the excitement of the large city are placing themselves in situations dangerous to their emotional and physical well-being without adequate ability to cope with these situations. Society, acting through the JJS, has a responsibility to assist such young children, at least in providing safe places for them to eat and sleep as well as opportunities for reuniting them with their families. As an example, many runaway shelters have served admirably within the JJS. To ask police agencies to provide such a service ignores the makeup of police agencies. If police agencies are required to handle such children, we can expect rather standard police procedures to be followed. Indeed, we might well be reluctant to permit police officers to counsel and guide such young children, since police officers usually have almost no training in such areas and have almost no automatic rapport with the kind of young children who run away. If the JJS is to have any measurable good impact on such children, the police must be taken out of the picture entirely.

RECOMMENDATION 10: THE JJS POLICE SHOULD NOT IN-
VESTIGATE, APPREHEND, COUNSEL, OR IN ANY WAY INTER-
ACT WITH DELINQUENT CHILDREN WHO HAVE NOT COM-
MITTED ACTS WHICH WOULD BE CRIMES IF COMMITTED BY
ADULTS.

One last police action problem or issue should be considered. This is
the special juvenile officer within the police agency who has particular
responsibility for juvenile cases. This special juvenile police officer may
have widely varying responsibilities within different police agencies,
including booking all juveniles, apprehending most juveniles, investigating
all reported status offenders, counseling all apprehended juveniles, working
closely with school counselors, and organizing baseball leagues (Portune,
1971). While many of these functions are valuable and can be beneficial
to children, the special juvenile police officer is an anachronism. As
urged above, police work within the JJS should be narrowly restricted to
criminal investigation, apprehension where necessary, and data gathering
and reporting. The very nature of the popularly accepted police role
within society makes the special juvenile police officer appear to be a fish
out of water.

Police agencies have tried to change their image, especially for the
younger audience (Pursuit, 1972). In many areas community relations
programs put police officers into classrooms to demonstrate their
humaneness and have police officers playing ball with children to show
they are "just one of the boys." While it is understandable for a police
officer to desire acceptance as a human being by the community in which
he lives, it is highly hypocritical and purposefully misleading to portray
the police officer as the friend of delinquent children. Society and the
JJS have designed fairly clear and unshakable roles for police officers
to play, and these roles clash directly with the police image as friend
of delinquents. Such efforts only further convince the delinquent child
of the hypocrisy of the JJS. Delinquent children know that your "friends"
don't arrest you or take you to jail; indeed, your "friends" would
normally help you avoid such consequences to the point of lying for you
or helping you escape from such a fate. Delinquent children perceive
perhaps more clearly than we do the repression and "occupying army"
attitude of many police officers, particularly in the parts of our cities
in which the large majority of delinquent children live. When "the man"
then comes into the neighborhood acting like a friend and a brother, he
loses any credibility he might have once had. If his job is unpopular but
at least he does it efficiently, honestly, and as humanely as possible, he
may earn the respect if not the admiration of those he serves. The special

juvenile police officer tends to reduce that respect considerably if he portrays a known punitive and repressive system as a humanistic and just system. Again, telling obvious lies to delinquent children about the JJS is the most damaging thing we can do.

RECOMMENDATION 11: THE JJS POLICE SHOULD NOT INCLUDE SPECIAL JUVENILE POLICE OFFICERS WITH OUTREACH OR COMMUNITY RELATIONS RESPONSIBILITIES BUT SHOULD LEAVE SUCH ACTIVITIES TO OTHER JJS AGENCIES.

JUVENILE COURT OPERATIONAL PROBLEMS AND RECOMMENDATIONS

Another category of JJS operational problems and issues is related to juvenile court operations. Of the six JJS subsystems described in chapter 3, the central four subsystems are controlled by juvenile courts and/or agents of juvenile courts. The juvenile court is clearly a power center of the JJS. Juvenile court agents—particularly the judge and probation officer—are the most influential agents within the JJS. Obviously, problems within this JJS agency can be critical to the successful functioning of the JJS.

Juvenile court judges occupy a pivotal position within the JJS. The verbal descriptions of persons needed for such positions, both historically and currently, represent the juvenile court judge as a person with all the virtues considered desirable in American life plus the legal skills of an expert trial lawyer plus the wisdom of Socrates. Not surprisingly, few juvenile court judges measure up to this ideal. One particular requirement or highly recommended characteristic is the root of a major issue or problem—the requirement that the juvenile court judge be a lawyer.

It is true that the juvenile court is a court and that the JJS is a legal system. Clearly, since *Gault* rather complex legal rules and procedures have governed the juvenile court. It would be quite difficult for someone untrained in law and trial procedures to conduct an adjudicatory hearing within the JJS. Even a large percentage of practicing lawyers would be unable to do so because of the somewhat rare legal specialty of juvenile law and particularly juvenile trial law. While a criminal trial lawyer could probably understand most juvenile proceedings, criminal trial lawyers make up a very small percentage of the bar.

To require that a juvenile court judge be a lawyer with trial experience is excellent but does not go far enough. A juvenile court judge needs abilities unlike those normally possessed by practicing lawyers or sitting judges. A juvenile court judge must have a basic understanding of social and behavioral sciences, particularly in such areas as the sociology of juvenile delinquency, child psychology, educational psychology, community social services, and public administration. The position of juvenile court judge is not filled adequately by a politically popular lawyer whose primary connections with children are his two middle class suburban children at home and the fact that he used to be a child himself. There is little reason to believe that the children he will see before the juvenile court will live in the kind of world in which he and his children live.

Research indicates that few juvenile court judges have the necessary broad background in social and behavioral sciences (Virijevich, 1976). Indeed, few potential judges (practicing lawyers with political connections) have significant training and abilities in areas other than law, business, and political science. As a result, solely law-trained juvenile court judges may tend to rely upon their juvenile probation officer for recommendations or, more frankly, decisions to be rubberstamped. This tendency informally but almost conclusively transfers judicial decision-making power to a person not appointed or elected to be a judge and someone who may well be an interested party in the litigation. No matter how capable the juvenile probation officer, it is highly inappropriate to assume one person can perform the vastly different and often clashing functions of probation officer and judge.

Ultimately, the juvenile court judge is assigned the JJS task of deciding the child's fate after considering legal, social science, and behavioral science evidence and information (Arthur, 1970). To avoid over-reliance on one source of such evidence and to provide the required check on the power of the juvenile probation officer, the juvenile court judge must be able to understand and consider this evidence independently. The juvenile court judge typically will not be able to pass on this task to a jury (McKeiver, 1971). Moreover, the decision as to the most appropriate disposition for a young, violent, first offender delinquent is perhaps more difficult than any other judicial decision in any legal system. Such a decision should not be based totally upon legal analysis or upon the recommendations of one social scientist. As long as the JJS continues to repose such awesome decisions in one person, society has a right to require that one person to be more than a trained lawyer.

RECOMMENDATION 12: THE JJS SHOULD REQUIRE THAT ALL JUVENILE COURT JUDGES HAVE ACADEMIC AND PRACTICAL TRAINING IN SOCIAL AND BEHAVIORAL SCIENCES DEALING WITH CHILDREN, IN ADDITION TO LEGAL TRAINING.

Another operational problem has to do with the probation officer acting as an investigator and preparer of social study reports for the juvenile court judge. The role of court investigator and gatherer of information for the judge is of critical importance. Juvenile court judges need as much information as possible concerning children before them. However, tradition, law, and system function limitations concerning the role of the juvenile court judge make it inappropriate and practically impossible for him to conduct investigations and go out into the community to inquire into a child's living situation and general social environment. Thus, judges must have these investigations conducted by someone else.

Juvenile courts can and do rely partly upon the two litigating parties in a delinquency case. The delinquent respondent's attorney can and should gather information to be presented as evidence favorable to the outcome and disposition desired by the child (Besharov, 1974). For example, if the child desires to be placed on official probation and allowed to live in his or her natural parents' home, the child's attorney presents evidence of the wholesomeness of the parents' home, the appropriateness of the supervision afforded by the parents, the beneficial effects of the neighborhood and peer group, etc. If the child desires placement in a group foster home, the child's attorney presents evidence of the home's desire to have the child as a resident, the good effects such a living situation would have on the child, the relatively bad effects living in the child's parents' home would have, the child's need for a large family-like setting, etc. In this manner the juvenile court judge is presented with substantial information concerning the child's needs, present living situation, and alternatives to the present situation. However, evidence presented by the child's attorney does not necessarily reveal all information relevant to the judge's decision.

The case's other litigant—the state—also presents evidence concerning the most appropriate disposition for the child. Such evidence necessarily involves information concerning the child's present and past living situation, family life, present and future environmental needs, etc. This evidence is based upon information gathered by the juvenile probation officer operating under the authority of the juvenile court and providing such information to the court as a comprehensive, objective social study report. In many jurisdictions the juvenile probation officer who conducts this pre-disposition social study is the same juvenile probation officer who brought the case to court originally (Teitelbaum, 1967).

Consider the personal situation of the juvenile probation officer. Often he is the person who first received the case at the juvenile court intake stage. After careful study of the case and often only after informal probation or other diversion has failed, the probation officer concludes that the case should go to formal court proceedings. From that conclusion alone it is clear that the probation officer does not believe that a relatively nonintrusive JJS action is appropriate. After the child is adjudicated delinquent and the time has come for the disposition to be imposed, the probation officer will seldom have changed his mind about the most appropriate disposition for this child. Thus, before the probation officer begins the social study investigation he has already prejudged the situation and at least tentatively decided upon the most appropriate disposition. Then the probation officer may conduct the social study investigation with an eye to gathering information to be used as evidence to support his prejudged recommendation.

The probation officer caught in this situation is no different from the researcher gathering data. It is very poor research methodology to decide first what position you wish your data to prove and then gather data to prove that position, carefully ignoring and/or denying the existence of data tending to cast doubt upon your position. Similarly, it is very poor JJS practice for a probation officer to decide first what disposition is appropriate and then gather information to support a prejudged recommendation, carefully ignoring and/or denying the existence of information tending to suggest the appropriateness of other dispositions. The social study investigation must be conducted by an objective investigator with no personal or professional stake in the investigation results. Therefore, the probation officer involved in the case up to the time of the social study investigation should not be permitted to conduct the social study investigation.

The solution to this problem is relatively simple for all but the smallest juvenile probation departments. Probation officers should be assigned limited tasks within the total probation function. Some officers would handle all intake cases, other officers would handle all social study investigations, and yet other officers would handle all probationer counseling. This arrangement avoids the problem of the probation officer who becomes personally and professionally attached to a case and then performs in an adversary role in juvenile court functions to achieve the end he desires. Of course, a major problem with this arrangement is the inability of a probation officer to understand a case fully if he is allowed to consider it only during a restricted time and for a restricted purpose. However, this is acceptable at the intake and social study investigation stages because an informed but objective decision is required. The probation officer can get deeply involved in the cases in which he is counseling probationers over a long period of time. Perhaps it would be best to assign all three functions to all probation officers but require different functions for different cases. That is, one probation officer would perform intake screening for children from A to H, perform social study investigations for children from I to Q, and serve as long-term counselor for children R to Z. Whatever the organization, it is a serious JJS error to allow the same probation officer to perform all three functions for the same child.

RECOMMENDATION 13: THE JJS SHOULD REQUIRE THAT DIFFERENT PERSONS CONDUCT INTAKE SCREENING HEARINGS, SOCIAL STUDY INVESTIGATIONS, AND LONG-TERM COUNSELING OF A PROBATIONER.

A final and most serious problem in JJS court operations is the lack of significant participation by prosecutors in juvenile court activities. Particularly since *Gault* in 1967 the presence of defense attorneys is a major factor in the entire JJS and particularly in juvenile court activities. As advocates for alleged delinquents, defense attorneys challenge the legality of court petitions, use legalistic tactics in response negotiations, prepare briefs on questions of law, interview and prepare witnesses for the child, cross-examine the petitioner and complaining witnesses, and generally see that the child's legal rights are protected (Besharov, 1974). In *Gault* the United States Supreme Court made clear the need for such attorneys for children in adjudicatory hearings and in the JJS under Fourteenth Amendment due process.

The delinquent respondent's attorney is an advocate for the child, skilled in legal tactics designed to convince the decision maker to adopt his view, or at least to affect the decision maker's decision. In a series of legal proceedings such as the constitutionalized JJS has become, such legal tactics are fundamental, and failure to understand them can be fatal. The constitutionalized JJS is an adversary system in classic Anglo-American tradition. As such, the participants are assumed to be skilled advocates capable of using the law and various legal strategies and tactics to influence the decisions of various juvenile justice decision makers. The child accused of delinquent conduct is represented by such an advocate. No requirement exists for a skilled advocate to represent the petitioner or the state.

Upon first consideration, the absence of skilled legal advocacy on behalf of the petitioner or state might seem to be to the advantage of the delinquent respondent. However, the absence of a prosecutor tends to seduce the juvenile court judge into playing the role of prosecutor (Besharov, 1974: 40-41). Few judges can remain aloof from the situation when a zealous attorney for the child elicits a one-sided development of the facts and law of a case with no countervailing activity on the prosecution side (Skoler, 1968).

For the judge to take up the role of the prosecutor can change the outcome of the entire hearing:

The assumption of a prosecutor's functions has a deep and subtle effect on a judge. He identifies himself with the cause for which he has labored; he grows to believe the evidence he has collected more than the juvenile's evidence. Having sought evidence against a juvenile, it becomes difficult for him to weigh it against the defense case dispassionately. If the judge becomes the advocate of the petitioner's case, he cannot keep an open mind until the moment of judgement and then sit back and apply the presumption of innocence as he considers all the evidence. (Besharov, 1974: 41)

Juvenile court judges, like almost all judges, are trained and experienced lawyers whose profession it is to advocate the position of their clients. This advocacy tradition is not easily put aside when one assumes a juvenile court judgeship. Much like the old firehorse that smells smoke, the juvenile court judge has difficulty avoiding the advocacy role, particularly when he sits by and watches a situation in which a much-needed advocacy role is not being filled.

The role of prosecutor is also needed at JJS junctures other than hearings. When the formal petition is being considered by the intake screening officer, that decision maker needs advice from an expert criminal lawyer as to the prosecutive merit of the case being considered. If the case is not provable in court, it is a costly and time-consuming error to file a formal petition in court. Whether or not a case is provable in court is often a difficult question requiring rather sophisticated knowledge of criminal and juvenile law, criminal and juvenile procedure, and the rules of evidence. Typically, only three JJS agents have such knowledge: the judge, the respondent's attorney, and the prosecutor. The juvenile court judge should not be asked to make such a decision because it can cause him to prejudge the case and asks him to assume trial tactics that he might use but that the person ultimately prosecuting the case might not wish to use. The respondent's attorney has obvious reasons to avoid commenting on the prosecutive merit of the case, other than vigorously to claim such merit to be nonexistent. The only proper source for such critically needed advice is the prosecutor.

Another JJS function needing the participation of the prosecutor is response negotiation ("plea bargaining"). This part of the proceedings is very seldom understood by persons other than trial attorneys. Response negotiation is shrouded in privacy and back room conversations, replete with assumptions, promises, threats, and accommodations between lawyers who at least tend to understand the ground rules. When a defense attorney becomes involved in response negotiations with nonlawyers, many of these tactics can be misunderstood, resulting in outcomes neither party expected or particularly desires. If response negotiation is to remain a part of the juvenile justice process (and there is no foreseeable point at which it will no longer exist), it should at least be conducted by skilled lawyer-negotiators equally matched and adequately representing both sides of the case.

Thus, prosecutors are critically needed within the JJS for filing petitions, response negotiation, and conducting hearings. The United States Supreme Court has required that children be represented at such points by competent attorneys. No such requirement has been made concerning prosecutors, leaving in most jurisdictions a most unfortunate situation in which juveniles' lawyers are matched against probation officers and police officers, judges are drawn into acting as prosecutors, and cases are brought into juvenile court which should have been dismissed for lack of evidence. Requiring prosecutors to represent the petitioners and the state at these points in the JJS would bring a degree of rationality and fairness to the system.

RECOMMENDATION 14: THE JJS SHOULD REQUIRE THE PROSECUTOR TO REPRESENT THE PETITIONER AT ALL CRITICAL STAGES WITHIN THE JJS.

JUVENILE CORRECTIONS OPERATIONAL PROBLEMS AND RECOMMENDATIONS

The area of juvenile corrections also reveals several operational problems and issues. One all-encompassing need is for the development and use of more information and reliable effectiveness measures for the various modes of juvenile corrections. Such effectiveness measures must begin with identification of the goals and objectives to be achieved. Goals such as "proper parenting" or "converting a delinquent child into a productive, law-abiding adult" are impressive but make establishment of effectiveness measures most difficult. Whether or not a given correctional technique provides "proper parenting" depends upon each person's perception of what "proper parenting" might be. To produce a "law-abiding adult" would seem to be a most difficult task in a society in which almost all adults violate laws.

Perhaps we should establish a simpler objective such as a reduction in the frequency and/or seriousness of delinquent acts by the subject child, tending toward an ultimate cessation in delinquent behavior. In the general deterrence area, one simple objective would be the reduction of the rate of actual occurrence of delinquent acts per one thousand children over a given period of time. Either desired result involves difficult data-access problems, since a child's actual activities are seldom well known and the total number of delinquent acts which occur has always been very difficult to ascertain. However, the JJS as a delinquency control sociolegal system should be evaluated on its ability to control delinquency, both for the individual child upon whom the JJS has had specific impact and for all children the JJS is empowered to affect.

The juvenile corrections area within the JJS has primary responsibility for the individual children assigned to various correctional modes for treatment. These correctional modes should be evaluated on their ability to reduce the frequency of delinquent acts of those specific children. Ideally, we need to be able accurately to forecast the probable frequency of future delinquent acts for a given child, assuming no "treatment" by juvenile corrections, and then be able to measure the actual frequency of delinquent acts for that child over a period of time subsequent to "treatment" by the JJS. A lower actual frequency of delinquent acts after treatment than had been forecast for the child without treatment might tend to indicate that the "treatment" was one of the causes of the lower frequency.

An equally important measure of effectiveness for juvenile correctional treatment would be a reduction in the seriousness or violent nature of the delinquent acts committed by a child subjected to such treatment. That is, a child adjudicated delinquent for habitual use of hard drugs who subsequently stops using hard drugs but switches to marijuana and beer, albeit at the same frequency of use, could be considered to have benefited from treatment. In making such evaluations we should not make all-or-nothing demands. Such effectiveness measures reveal disastrous naiveté concerning the general petty lawlessness of the American population. We should ask delinquent children to become no better than the rest of us, and thus replace their more shocking and threatening lawlessness with the more acceptable petty lawlessness of the rest of us.

Development of such effectiveness measures will of course take some time and effort on the part of scholars and practitioners in juvenile justice. Forecasts of frequency and nature of probable future delinquent acts can be based partly upon past behavior, but much more accurate forecasting abilities are needed. Revelation of actual frequency and nature of delinquent acts subsequent to treatment is dependent upon our ability to ascertain the actual occurrence of delinquent acts and identify the perpetrator of those acts.

In addition to these technical problems, a major depreciating factor in the value of these effectiveness measures is the tendency of the juvenile correctional modes to "filter" the data before it is reported. That is, group foster home X may have a tendency to forecast a high probable rate of future delinquent acts of grave seriousness for new residents. Then, when we later observe a somewhat lower rate of delinquent acts of less than grave seriousness, we conclude that group foster home X has had a significantly beneficial effect upon the residents. However, group foster home X might have a tendency to underreport the occurrence of actual acts of delinquency known to them to have been committed by present or past residents of the home, thus making it appear that the home's products are behaving better than they actually are. These tendencies, by no means limited to group foster homes, result in comparisons between unrealistically inflated forecasts and very conservative reports of subsequent behavior. Such results make impressive claims for correctional modes seeking continued funding or greater recognition but are not helpful for those interested in achievement of JJS goals and objectives. Development of effectiveness measures must include means of objectively forecasting probable behavior and truthfully reporting actual behavior.

RECOMMENDATION 15: THE JJS SHOULD DEVELOP RELIABLE MEANS FOR MEASURING THE TENDENCY OF VARIOUS CORRECTIONAL MODES TO REDUCE THE FREQUENCY AND/OR SERIOUSNESS OF DELINQUENT ACTS COMMITTED BY CHILDREN SUBJECTED TO SUCH CORRECTIONAL MODES.

In addition to effectiveness measures for treatment programs, the JJS needs more authentic attempts at appropriate treatment for delinquency problems. Admittedly, we need to know much more about effective treatment techniques for delinquency, but one immediate improvement would be to implement universally what knowledge we have, or openly admit our ignorance and not simply "look busy." The delinquent's legal right to treatment is beginning to force such action upon the JJS (Kittrie, 1969). It is embarrassing that JJS treatment personnel must be ordered by a court of law to offer treatment (Pyfer, 1972).

It is not suggested that experimental and unproven treatment modes be imposed upon delinquent children. On the contrary, treatment modes for delinquent children should be the least intrusive possible and should be carefully limited to a few select children until proved reasonably effective and unharmful to children (Kittrie, 1971). However, many juvenile correction activities are remarkably devoid of any meaningful attempt at treatment in situations in which some attempts at treatment are possible.

For example, juvenile institutions should be more than a place to house children securely for a period of time before releasing them back into society. Regardless of the long-standing debate over the value of juvenile institutions, such juvenile corrections modes are a part of the JJS in almost all jurisdictions, and finding alternatives—particularly for the violent child—will require much more than the phethora of vehement rhetoric about the evils of such institutions. Until less objectionable and more humane alternatives are developed, institutions will continue to exist and can offer some basic forms of "treatment."

The institution can offer regular—ideally, daily—counseling to each incarcerated child. The goal of such counseling may be simply to tend to offset the innately destructive nature of institutionalization and to keep the child in at least minimal contact with human beings. Such counseling would not be intensive psychotherapy but simply daily conversations, individual and group, on a friendly, informal basis. Perhaps such counseling should not be referred to as "treatment" but nevertheless should be a fixed part of juvenile institution programs. Such counseling could significantly blunt the tendency of institutions to convert misbehaving children into hostile adult criminals.

Juvenile institutions can also make available to all incarcerated children access to books, television, sports equipment, and the other trappings of normal American teenage life. While institutions proudly display such equipment, it is often vastly restricted in quantity and quality and is denied to many of the children for purposes of punishment for infractions of rules. As with informal counseling, perhaps such facilities cannot properly be called treatment, but neither can denial of such facilities be called treatment.

The juvenile probation area is not immune from this problem. At a minimum, juvenile probation officers should be available for counseling or informal "rap sessions" on a regular basis and at times more convenient for the probationers, such as evenings and weekends. Juvenile probation officers can actively seek meaningful jobs for their probationers from public-minded local employers, organize summer and weekend activities for probationers, and generally make community resources more available to delinquent probationers than they are for other children. Juvenile probation officers should help the child cope with the real world rather than simply watch over him and report missteps to the court. Perhaps again this is not actually treatment, but it does seem to be much more in line with the JJS goals and objectives.

These authentic attempts at appropriate treatment would require increased funding and personnel in various juvenile correction agencies. In many cases the lack of treatment is not the fault of the agency or agents, who would like nothing more than to be able to offer such things to children in their care. However, the funding levels and caseloads of such agencies effectively prevent such programs (Midoneck and Besharov, 1972). We then come to the desire of governmental spending entities to provide authentic attempts at appropriate treatment for delinquent children. In effect, it comes down to the American government's willingness to match JJS treatment rhetoric with JJS treatment programs and the American people's desire to take reasonable steps to combat present juvenile delinquency and future adult crime.

RECOMMENDATION 16: THE JJS SHOULD BE PROVIDED SUFFICIENT FUNDS TO SUPPORT AUTHENTIC ATTEMPTS AT MINIMUM INTERVENTION TREATMENT PROGRAMS FOR DELINQUENCY.

Another operational problem in juvenile corrections is the vast, almost unchecked discretion of the juvenile probation officer. This JJS agent has wide-ranging effects on the clients of the JJS, in that he often enters the case soon after an act of delinquency is reported and typically has effective control over the case during intake screening, petition filing, diversion to the informal JJS, and the dispositional stages.

The exercise of this discretionary authority is generally unchecked by the juvenile probation officer's employer, the juvenile court judge. Juvenile court judges tend to assign many tasks to their probation officers but do not have the time or inclination to supervise their activities closely. Moreover, juvenile probation officers are qualified professionals assumed capable of performing their duties with minimum supervision by employers. Suggestions that such professionals should restrict their activities are likely to fall on deaf ears. Juvenile probation officers typically believe quite fervently in their attempts to help children they perceive to be in need of help. They tend to work long hours for relatively low pay and find the children's appreciation of their efforts to be rare. Like police, they may feel "handcuffed" by the law's procedural requirements and prevented from carrying out fully their humanitarian missions.

One problem resulting from this unchecked discretion is overreaching by the probation officer into functions not properly performed by him. Probation officers, like almost all JJS professionals, tend to want to act as judges, or at least assume the powers of judges. That is, probation officers often want to go beyond counseling children and investigation of the social environment of children. They may tend to decide in their own mind whether or not the child committed the delinquent act, whether or not the child is in need of treatment, and what dispositional alternative would be most appropriate for the child. These decisions are often made by probation officers as well as prosecutors, juveniles' attorneys, police, and other JJS agents.

Once the juvenile probation officer has decided in his own mind what the proper result for a case is, he is no longer an objective investigator and counselor but is an advocate for his personal conclusions and overly critical of other alternatives. Caught up in the adversary setting of the JJS, the probation officer sees all other players advocating their pet theories and thus may tend to become an unobjective advocate for his pet theory.

The juvenile probation officer is one of the least objective JJS agents; yet objectivity is an essential quality for JJS decision makers. Lack of objectivity is particularly obvious in cases involving repeated offenses, earnest counseling after each offense, and a substantial investment of personal effort and concern by the juvenile probation officer. It is not surprising that the probation officer may tend to personalize the child's persistent misbehavior and react in a human and nonobjective manner by seeking to punish the child for rejection of his "parental" efforts. This is child abuse by the "governmental parent" and is caused largely by the same factors as child abuse by natural parents. One repeatedly, patiently, and lovingly tries to reform the child's irritating misbehavior, and finally, out of frustration, one lashes out to punish and hurt the child in revenge for the hurt caused by the child (Walters, 1975). Here the governmental parent, through the juvenile probation officer, tries repeatedly in a nice way to change the child's behavior and is no less immune to frustration and anger when the child defiantly rejects the attempts.

Many other examples could be cited. The conclusion must be that to permit unchecked and effectively unsupervised activity by any JJS agent is unwise, particularly for a JJS agent with as much power over children's lives as is exercised by juvenile probation officers. This is not to say that juvenile probation officers are generally unqualified, uncaring, or naturally bent upon destroying children's lives. To place fairly tight controls upon JJS agents performing a most humanitarian task is not a novel idea, since this was the thrust of *Gault*'s proceduralizing of the juvenile court judge's functions. We simply should agree that unchecked discretion and power is always potentially subject to abuse and should be designed out of the system whenever possible. As with recommendation 8 above, the juvenile probation officer should not be asked or permitted to be all things to all people.

RECOMMENDATION 17: THE JJS ROLE OF JUVENILE PRO-
BATION OFFICER SHOULD BE MORE RESTRICTIVELY
DESIGNED, WITH ACTIVE SUPERVISION OF ALL ACTIVITIES
AND WRITTEN JUSTIFICATION FOR ALL DECISIONS.

One last juvenile corrections operational problem is of interest. Regardless of the purpose of, reasons for, and debate about juvenile correctional institutions, a major JJS operational problem is the harm to children inflicted by such institutions during day-to-day operations (Scott and Hissong, 1969). Of concern here is the specific harm resulting from operations of the institutions, not the also important questions of the role of institutions in corrections, the appropriateness of institutions for certain classes of offenders, the debate over small vs. large institutions, etc.

A persuasive argument can be made that all children forced to reside in juvenile corrections institutions are unavoidably harmed continuously and irreparably by the institution. Such unavoidable harms stem from the essentially antihuman nature of any large, bureaucratic institution, the emotionally and physically damaging acts committed against them by custodians and other children in the institution, the unrealistic day-to-day routine of the institution, the denial of regular contacts with the general society, etc. While these harms cannot be totally avoided as long as children are institutionalized, they can be reduced, and means can be provided to the children to recover from the harm once they are released.

At the outset those JJS agents responsible for the day-to-day operations of the institution should recognize and admit the unavoidable harm caused by institutionalization. As a result, they should develop programs within the institution and the aftercare programs to blunt the effect of that harm. Counseling can include frank discussions with the child about the problems of life in an institution and tactics for coping with such problems. Extra care can be exercised to insure that children incarcerated in institutions are kept as busy in meaningful activities as possible and have as much contact as possible with persons on the outside. Such children should be kept well informed as to changing styles, interests, and opinions of their contemporaries on the outside. Visits to their homes or other noninstitution places should be as frequent and as extensive as possible. In general, life in the institution should be made as non-institutional as possible.

A premise here is that institutionalization of delinquent children is justifiable only in order to protect the general public. Institutionalization is not intended to punish the child or to be a particular deprivation of privileges for the child. The sole justification for juvenile institutions is that some children may be too destructive to be allowed freedom until that destructive behavior can be modified (Eldefonso and Hartinger, 1976: 281). Day-to-day operations of the institutions should reflect this premise and impose no more restrictions and unnatural limitations on the child than are absolutely necessary because of the child's destructive nature. Moreover, such restrictions and limitations should never be used as punishment or disciplinary tactics within institutions.

RECOMMENDATION 18: THE JJS SHOULD OPENLY RECOG-NIZE THE UNAVOIDABLE HARM CAUSED TO CHILDREN BY JUVENILE INSTITUTIONS AND MAKE EVERY ATTEMPT TO COUNTERACT SUCH HARM THROUGH PROACTIVE AND REACTIVE COUNSELING, A VARIETY OF NEAR-NORMAL ACTIVITIES, AND AS MUCH CONTACT WITH THE OUTSIDE COMMUNITY AS POSSIBLE.

6. JJS EFFECTS

PROBLEMS AND RECOMMENDATIONS

In addition to problems resulting primarily from JJS philosophy, design, and operations, additional problems have more to do with unintended effects of the JJS. These inappropriate effects or results are in many cases surprising and not at all what would normally be expected from cursory analysis of the JJS. Nevertheless, counterproductive effects must be recognized and dealt with if possible.

JJS UNDESIRABLE EFFECTS ON CHILDREN

Laws defining delinquent acts and the procedural techniques used in handling delinquent children may tend to delay maturation of those children and tend to teach them to avoid responsibility for their actions. Our laws categorically state that persons under a certain age, from sixteen to eighteen, are not legally responsible for their actions in the same way as adults. JJS procedures clearly require JJS agents to process children in a different, condescending manner, constantly reminding delinquent children that they are too immature to be treated as adults (Forer, 1970).

One effect of this treatment of delinquent children may be to tend to encourage them to remain "emotional children." This effect is unfortunate for delinquent children aged fifteen to eighteen who live in those parts of our society which are particularly unprotective to anyone, including children. The JJS seems to envision the world of children as like that portrayed by television and movies for middle class, rural, or small-town families who work hard, spend lavish amounts of time together, and seem to be able to help their children through a variety of minor mishaps. That this portrayal is inaccurate for many delinquent children is apparent. However, the JJS effect on delinquent children can be to persuade them that several capable adults care about them and will fend off problems for them, allowing them to grow up at their own pace.

This is misleading and a disservice to delinquent children. Consider children who have been labeled "delinquent" by the JJS and at the age of sixteen or seventeen must live in the less pleasant parts of our cities, must be the oldest male in the household, and must work if possible to help support the family unit. It is destructive in their situation to cause them to believe they may act irresponsibly and not be held accountable or that they may turn to a caring, omniscient adult to solve problems they find too difficult. It would be much better to assist them in more fully assuming the adult role into which they have been prematurely thrust and have no option but to carry out.

As an example of this effect, consider the juvenile institution or other correctional program which focuses upon improving the delinquent child's functioning in a public school setting, teaching a better attitude for a young child in relating to parental requests, and the inculcation of a myriad of other appropriate behavior patterns for young children according to the American ideal. Many if not most of these delinquent children have long since passed through that stage of life and will never again play the role of the young child. Regardless of their chronological age, they now have only one role available, and that is as an adult with adult responsibilities. It would seem to be much more appropriate to teach them necessary adult skills such as adult interpersonal relationships, employment skills, the handling of opportunities for abuse of drugs or for other potentially detrimental diversions, and the general nature of the world as those "adult-children" will know it.

This effect is not limited to delinquent children but may also persuade nondelinquent children that they may act irresponsibly up until age eighteen. It is obviously detrimental to the child who wishes to go on to college or engage in any other postchildhood activity for which one must substantially prepare as a child. Particularly for the older child but also for all children, the JJS should try to produce the effect of encouraging responsible and thoughtful behavior. No children, delinquent or nondelinquent, older or younger, should be taught that violent assault and battery or rape are permissible if you are below a legal age limit. It seems apparent that the JJS does not intend to teach this, but the JJS can and does have that effect on some children.

RECOMMENDATION 19: THE JJS SHOULD IMPRESS UPON ALL CHILDREN THE NEED FOR RESPONSIBLE AND MATURE

BEHAVIOR AND PREPARE CHILDREN FOR THEIR FUTURE AS ADULTS AS WELL AS THEIR PRESENT STATUS AS CHILDREN.

Another unfortunate effect of the JJS on children is to tend to deny their individuality and impose one "correct" mode of behavior on all children. By listing the primary forbidden behavior modes in our laws defining acts of delinquency, we have greatly narrowed the range of possible behavior patterns children might choose.

By declaring delinquent all acts which would be crimes if committed by adults, we make it clear that criminal acts are not a permissible behavior pattern. It is assumed that few would disagree with this, except for the points raised in the discussion preceding recommendation 6 above. However, many noncriminal acts are also forbidden to children by being designated as acts of delinquency.

It is an act of delinquency to be habitually truant from school unless the child is over the minimum age. Thus, a behavior pattern which does not include regular attendance at school is forbidden to children. In many jurisdictions a child is not only required by law to attend school but is required by aggressive probation officers and social workers to study hard and do well in school, with the ultimate mark of achievement being a decision to go to college. The child is not permitted, by law and/or by counseling, to adopt a behavior pattern which rejects formal schooling and instead seeks experiential education, working at low-skilled occupations, and generally following a lower class lifestyle.

Another example of a denied behavior pattern is the tendency to run away from home and travel from town to town with no particular stability in one's activities. This behavior pattern is denied to children by laws which make running away an act of delinquency and by JJS counselors who demand regularity, dependability, and predictability in behavior. Laws declaring delinquent the phenomenon of "growing up in idleness" obviously have this effect.

All laws, particularly criminal and juvenile laws, have as a fundamental purpose the denial of certain behavior patterns. However, the JJS denies some behavior patterns which not all concerned persons would agree should be forbidden to human beings, including children. Has formal schooling as it exists in America had such an outstanding record that we can justify forcing all Americans to participate therein, regardless of their desires? Is the phenomenon of the carefree, rootless drifter so threatening to our society that we must deny this alternative to our children? It might be suggested that we have considerable disagreement as to the notion of the "correct" child or the "correct" adult. The JJS produces the effect of denying to our children several patterns of behavior which are simply unpopular with the legislatures in our society and which are not necessarily a threat to our society or justifiably a concern of our society.

RECOMMENDATION 20: THE JJS SHOULD AMEND ITS LAWS AND ACTIONS SO AS TO ENCOURAGE A WIDE RANGE OF BEHAVIOR PATTERNS FOR CHILDREN, BOUNDED ONLY BY OUR CRIMINAL LAWS.

In effect, the JJS also tends to lead our children to deny facts they know to be true. If a child commits an act of delinquency and openly admits the offense to JJS authorities, that child is much more likely to be processed and thus punished by the JJS than if he had not admitted the facts. If the child is investigated for having committed an act of delinquency and refuses to tell the truth about the incident, the chances of formal adjudication for that offense are reduced greatly. All defense attorneys know, and our children quickly learn, that refusal to cooperate with the police in investigating an offense greatly reduces the probability that the police will be able to gather sufficient evidence to make a case in court.

Consider the self-preservation motives of the child. He has committed an act of delinquency. The act has been discovered and is being investigated by JJS authorities. The child knows, and is reminded by his attorney, that telling the truth about the matter to JJS agents might make him feel better. However, it will greatly increase the probability of a legal case being made against him and thus of his being adjudicated delinquent and receiving a formal disposition. If he agrees to cooperate with JJS authorities and tells the truth, he may avoid formal adjudication but will receive almost the same disposition through the informal JJS. It comes down to the possibility of having disposition X imposed, formally or informally. Regardless of the rhetoric of the JJS, few dispositions are pleasant for or are desired by the child. The child typically wishes to avoid such dispositions. The effect of the JJS is to tell the child that avoiding the truth is the best means of avoiding the disposition and that telling the truth is the worst means of avoiding the disposition.

This situation is somewhat like that of the child caught by his mother after a theft from the cookie jar, with one significant difference. The cookie thief may perceive that his mother believes he is guilty and will administer her "disposition" regardless of his admissions. If he does not perceive this, he may try to lie his way out of it. If his mother has made fairly conclusive presumptions of guilt, then telling the truth may reduce the severity of the punishment. But either way, the child has no means of preventing the disposition from being administered.

The child accused of delinquency does have substantial means for preventing the disposition from being administered. The child can refuse to cooperate and thus avoid the informal JJS. He will then be subject only to the formal JJS and can lie or at least refuse to tell the truth and thus greatly reduce the chance of a disposition being imposed. The JJS, unlike his mother, cannot impose a disposition without substantial proof ("beyond a reasonable doubt") in cases involving criminal acts. Thus, while lying only occasionally avoids mother's wrath, lying can be a very effective means of avoiding a JJS disposition.

The only effective method of avoiding this disastrous JJS effect is to refuse to allow the child to make denials or admissions at all. Require the JJS to prove the case from beginning to end without assistance from the child, which is a fundamental meaning of the Fifth Amendment's privilege against self-incrimination. The possible assistance the child's statements might contribute is far outweighed by the pressure we are putting on the child to lie. Until means are discovered for effectively rewarding a child for telling the truth, the JJS should strenuously avoid the effect of encouraging a child to lie.

RECOMMENDATION 21: THE JJS SHOULD NOT PERMIT SUSPECTED DELINQUENTS TO MAKE ANY STATEMENT TO JJS AGENTS ABOUT THE CASE BEING INVESTIGATED UNLESS AND UNTIL THE CHILD IS ADJUDICATED DE-LINQUENT BY THE JUVENILE COURT.

Even worse than encouraging children to lie is the tendency of the JJS to cause future delinquency in children who come into contact with the JJS (Dilemma, 1972). This unfortunate JJS effect comes about when children guilty of minor misbehavior come into contact with and under the influence of children who have been and will be engaged in much more serious, perhaps criminal, behavior (Scott and Hissong, 1969). Consider the small-town child institutionalized for truancy and disobedience. He becomes acquainted with other children in the institution, many of whom have been involved in burglary, car theft, and drug offenses. Upon release from the institution the small-town child has a much wider range of delinquent possibilities and may have become a habitual user of illegal drugs while in the institution. This child's subsequent delinquent acts can be said to have been caused at least partly by the JJS. If the JJS had never intervened in his life and certainly if he had never been placed in a juvenile institution, the child would have been much less likely to commit those particular serious acts of delinquency and probably less likely to commit any future acts of delinquency.

Consider a similar pattern resulting from detention in a local jail pending various JJS procedures. The child incarcerated in a jail may come into contact with persons in that jail who expose the child to patterns of behavior unknown to the child previously. Might it also be that the very fact of being incarcerated, regardless of contact with other prisoners, would tend to make the child more hostile toward society and more resolved to commit antisocial acts in the role of delinquent child that the JJS has assigned to him? This would seem to be particularly true for the confused child seeking an identity and role in life. Perhaps the JJS is providing an identity and role for such a child—that of delinquent child and apprentice to the role of criminal adult (Cicourel, 1968).

Another way in which the JJS tends to cause future delinquency lies in the definition of delinquency. Delinquent children are those children who violate laws defining delinquent acts and who are caught and adjudicated delinquent because of those acts. Children already processed by the JJS previously are more likely to be caught for subsequent acts of delinquency than children never processed by the JJS (Langley, 1972). This is for several reasons, including police watchfulness over previously delinquent children, the willingness of school officials and neighbors to report the delinquent acts of previously delinquent children, and the juvenile prosecutor's willingness to prosecute second and third offenders. Given the same number of subsequent delinquent acts as other children not previously exposed to the JJS, the previously delinquent child may well have a higher probability of apprehension, prosecution, and adjudication (Blinick, 1968). But for having been declared delinquent in the past, he might not have been declared delinquent now. In that sense, previous action by the JJS has been one of the causes of the present delinquency.

One solution to this problem that should be given more consideration is simply to abolish the JJS and thus avoid the possibility of the JJS ever having any contact with any children. If the JJS did not exist, it could not be a cause of future delinquency. Bolstering this argument is the fact that almost all "law-abiding" adults committed acts of delinquency as children, never came to the attention of the JJS, and then tended to cease this delinquent behavior as they matured. Conversely, a large percentage of adult criminals did come to the attention of the JJS as a result of their delinquent acts and did not cease the delinquent behavior as they matured.

It is precisely such phenomena as these that give rise to searches for cause-and-effect relationships. A more pragmatic approach would be to ask the JJS to understand this unfortunate effect and act to blunt it wherever possible.

RECOMMENDATION 22: THE JJS SHOULD AVOID EXPOSING LESS SERIOUS OFFENDERS TO MORE SERIOUS OFFENDERS AND AVOID THE TENDENCY TO TREAT PREVIOUSLY DE-LINQUENT CHILDREN MORE HARSHLY AND SUSPICIOUSLY DURING PRE-DISPOSITIONAL PHASES OF THE JJS.

RECOMMENDATION 22A: AMERICAN SOCIETY SHOULD SERIOUSLY CONSIDER ABOLISHING THE JJS, AS A PRIMARY CAUSE OF DELINQUENCY.

A very serious societal effect of the JJS is the tendency to oppress all children as a class within American society. By singling out all persons under a certain age and subjecting this group to a different, less generous set of rights than the rest of society, we are purposely and knowingly discriminating against that class of people. Of course, almost all American legal systems do this in that children are not allowed to vote, own property, get married, consume alcohol, etc. At this point in our history we have removed much unfair legal discrimination against other classes, the most prominent current examples being black people and women. However, a comparable and often more oppressive discrimination against children has not been generally recognized as objectionable or unfair, and few steps have been taken to reduce this discrimination.

The JJS and the criminal justice system are not permitted to be sexist or racist but are permitted to be "ageist." Indeed, discrimination based upon the age of the offender is the primary premise of the JJS/CJS bifurcation. The resulting effect of JJS existence and operation is to single out one class of persons in our society for special attention, such attention including punishment of behaviors not punishable for any other class, dispositional modes not allowed for any other class, and governmental intervention in a child's life for a longer period of time than would be permissible for any other class for many offenses.

As a result, children may rightfully perceive themselves as an oppressed class and thus feel less allegiance to the rest of society. They are likely to interpret the assertion that they are simply being protected by the rest of us in the same way that assertion was interpreted by southern blacks when made by their white oppressors and by women when made by their male oppressors. America has a tradition in which the group in power justifies its elitist position and discrimination against other groups by claiming it is only protecting the oppressed classes from various evils and hazards. Blacks, women, and other oppressed groups have now seen through this rhetoric, and it seems likely that children will soon do likewise.

This JJS effect could be disastrous in that it could cause tension and distrust between children and adults. Moreover, much of this class oppression is unnecessary. Few would argue that five-year-old children should be given legal rights comparable to those of an adult, but can we come to such an easy conclusion concerning the comparison between seventeen-year-old working husband/fathers and twenty-two-year-old college seniors? Perhaps the legal rights applicable should be determined by a formula which includes age, primary activity, educational level, maturity, and other factors. Is it appropriate for our law to state categorically that all seventeen-year-olds are conclusively presumed to be less mature and responsible than all eighteen-year-olds?

The JJS should recognize this tendency to discriminate in a manner detrimental toward all children as a minority class in our society. In an attempt to reduce this class discrimination, all special treatment of children should be reviewed in order to determine if it is absolutely necessary for the JJS to function. Obvious candidates for in-depth review are the denial to children of adult rights to bail and jury trials, as well as longer incarceration of children than of adults for the same offense. Indeed, this inquiry quickly leads to an investigation of the reason for the separation of the children's JJS from the adult CJS.

RECOMMENDATION 23: THE JJS SHOULD EXAMINE ALL SPECIAL LAWS AND PROCEDURES FOR CHILDREN AND DISCARD AS MANY AS POSSIBLE IN AN ATTEMPT TO RE-DUCE DISCRIMINATION AGAINST CHILDREN AS A CLASS.

In addition to the JJS effect of discriminating against children as a class, another JJS effect is to bolster and reenforce class division and hatred among all children. Since all children commit acts of delinquency but only some children are selected to be processed by the JJS, this differential treatment of certain groups of children can tend to lead those groups of children to harbor resentment toward their treatment, and envy plus some dislike for those groups of children ignored by the JJS. If one were black, poor, doing poorly in school, *and* were continually harassed by the JJS for delinquent acts, anger might be an understandable reaction toward those children who were white, not poor, and doing well in school, particularly if they were not harassed by the JJS for their delinquent acts. Conversely, the privileged group of children might conclude from the actions of the JJS that the other group of children must somehow deserve the JJS harassment because of some inherent evilness or tendency to be a threat to society. In this way the JJS passes on the class prejudices and hatreds which permeate the adult world.

We must not mistake this encouraged turmoil among our children as being between children who commit acts of delinquency and children who do not commit acts of delinquency. A premise of this entire JJS analysis is that virtually all children commit acts of delinquency but only a small percentage of all children are selected for processing by the JJS. It is this racially and culturally prejudiced selection process that tends to pass along these racial and cultural prejudices to our children. As a result, we have encouraged animosity between children who commit delinquent acts but don't get caught and children who commit delinquent acts and do get caught.

As long as substantial discretion is exercised by JJS agents and those agents are hired from a pool of candidates who are racially and culturally prejudiced, this unfortunate JJS effect will continue. Although a dream of many social analysts, the removal of racial and cultural prejudice from our society is far from accomplished and will not be accomplished in the near future. Perhaps we cannot keep natural parents from passing along their prejudices to their children, but we should be able to keep the government parent from doing so. The primary means of accomplishing this will be to greatly reduce the exercise of discretion within the JJS.

This reduction of discretion would mean apprehension of or summoning all children suspected of delinquent behavior, with no discretion to screen out those children who don't appear to need the services of the JJS. All children would be dismissed, shunted into the informal JJS, or referred to juvenile court according to an objective point scale with little leeway for personal judgment. Similar restriction on all personal discretion would characterize the entire system. To have to remove such a fundamental factor as professional discretion from the JJS is unfortunate, but the alternative is to pass along racial and cultural prejudices and hatreds which are much more unfortunate for society.

RECOMMENDATION 24: THE JJS SHOULD GREATLY RE- DUCE THE DISCRETION OF ALL ITS AGENTS IN ORDER TO REDUCE THE TENDENCY TO INCULCATE RACIAL AND CULTURAL PREJUDICES IN CHILDREN.

JJS UNDESIRABLE EFFECTS ON SOCIETY

In addition to the undesirable effects described above, other factors have a broader effect on society. Of course, children are a part of society, but these effects are not limited to or particularly burdensome for children in the society. These undesirable effects involve unforeseen impacts on the parent-child relationship and an unrealistic sense of security for a crime-fearing public.

In many JJS situations the parents and their children are cast in adversary roles and are required by the JJS to engage in verbal and intellectual combat against each other. This is particularly true in cases of alleged incorrigibility, fugitive, and similar charges. If the child's alleged delinquent acts consist of habitually disobeying his parents or being beyond their control, the primary witness for the state against the alleged delinquent child will be the parent. Consider the scenario in which the apprehensive child sits through a formalistic, somewhat traumatic court procedure during which several authoritarian adults are explaining in detail the child's misbehavior. What is the impact on the child if the primary accuser before this awesome tribunal is his own parent? The ultimate emotional twist for the child may come when the child's attorney strenuously cross-examines the parent, using information obtained from the child to catch the parent in an exaggeration or perhaps a false statement. Although this confrontation may last less than an hour, the destructive impact on the future relationship of that parent and child can be permanent. A shocking sequel comes after the child is adjudicated delinquent when various JJS agents work to strengthen the parent-child relationship which the adjudicatory process has just finished damaging, perhaps irreparably.

This parent-child clash typically occurs during conferences with probation officers and at adjudicatory hearings in juvenile court. While various techniques can be employed in informal conferences to avoid at least the most damaging effects of such clashes, the very nature of adversary proceedings in court makes avoidance more difficult. Particularly since *Gault* an adversary proceeding is required, and fairly traditional Anglo-American legal roles are played. The prosecutor presents evidence tending to prove the child's delinquency and the child's attorney challenges that evidence. Then the child's attorney presents evidence refuting the prosecutor's evidence and the prosecutor challenges that evidence. Often the key evidence on either side will be oral testimony by the parent and/or child as to the specific disobedient acts or the specific indications that the child is beyond the control of the parent. Rules of evidence and procedural law will not normally permit other kinds of evidence to be substituted for this oral testimony and tend to require that such testimonial evidence be detailed and specific, with few embarrassing details omitted. Thus, even when the parent and/or the child wish to downplay or soften this clash, juvenile law will not permit them to do so. The only available means of avoiding this clash is to avoid bringing the case to juvenile court.

The reasons behind this requirement of adversary procedure are valid. The state should not be able to label a child "delinquent" and impose severe sanctions on that child without substantial, trustworthy information indicating his delinquency. The JJS cannot simply accept the unsubstantiated allegations of an angry, frustrated parent seeking the assistance of the JJS in disciplining a recalcitrant child. Neither can the JJS simply accept a child's denial of delinquent behavior without supporting information, at least until that day when all children in our society always tell the truth.

A modification to the purely adversary proceeding suggests itself. While continuing to use oral testimony by the parent and the child in adversary hearings, the JJS could require that such testimony be given in closed session without the other party personally present. That is, when the parent is testifying the child would be represented by his attorney, but the child would not personally be present. Similarly, when the child is testifying the parents would be represented by the prosecutor and their private attorney, but the parents would not personally be present. This would retain the fundamental right to confront and cross-examine witnesses but would significantly reduce the trauma and negative impact on the parent-child relationship. Of course, the JJS agents who were present during such testimony in closed sessions would have to avoid later revealing the substance of that testimony to the other party, or the benefits from such a scheme would be largely lost.

RECOMMENDATION 25: THE JJS SHOULD REQUIRE THAT ORAL TESTIMONY BY PARENTS OR CHILDREN WHICH IS DETRIMENTAL TO THE PARENT-CHILD RELATIONSHIP BE RESTRICTED TO CLOSED SESSIONS IN WHICH THE OTHER PARTY IS NOT PRESENT BUT IS REPRESENTED BY COUNSEL.

Another detrimental effect on the parent-child relationship can be the tendency of the JJS to reenforce questionable parental practices. The essential nature of the JJS is to be a conservative, nonpermissive, potentially punitive parental model which can be used to back up natural parents who exhibit the same characteristics. A teenager's natural parents or foster parents can absolutely forbid any activity outside the home except school, and in some cases private tutoring can be substituted for public schooling. That is, the teenager can be forbidden by his or her parents to date, go to ballgames or parties, go shopping, ride a bicycle, sit in the back yard, etc. If such extreme rules are broken by the teenager several times, the basis is formed for a provable allegation of habitual disobedience. The teenager can be adjudicated a delinquent child under habitual disobedience statutes in many jurisdictions and has no strong legal defense. As long as the parents' orders are not illegal or perhaps immoral, the JJS will stand behind the parents.

Many statutes defining delinquency or "persons in need of supervision" include terms such as "incorrigible," "ungovernable," "habitually disobedient," "runaway," and similar indications of noncompliance with parental wishes. All these terms refer to repeated incidents of the parents' or guardians' ordering the child to perform or refrain from performing an act, to which orders the child responds by performing inadequately according to the parent or guardian. Of course, the implication is that the parental orders will be reasonable, but juvenile law is conspicuously silent concerning this. The tradition of criminal law is explicitly and narrowly to set forth the prohibited acts so that all will be aware of the prohibitions and either avoid the prohibited acts or transgress at their own risk. The opposite seems to be true about this area of juvenile law.

Consider the opposite extreme in parental behavior. Parents who are permissive and prohibit very few activities for their children are not reenforced by the JJS. No juvenile laws force parents to let their children have more freedom, except for child abuse cases in which, for example, the child is locked in the basement. Parents do not bring their children into juvenile court complaining that the children don't go out enough or that they obey parental requests too often. No social control system—law-based or nonlaw-based—stands behind that variety of parental control. The JJS seems to reenforce the parent who demands strict compliance with parental directives and the child who refuses to reach out to a variety of behavior patterns or to unconventional activities.

This JJS analysis cannot discuss in detail the controversy concerning strict parenting versus permissive parenting. It is simply suggested that the JJS reenforces strict—sometimes overly strict—parenting but militates against more permissive parenting. If the parents are too permissive and permit their children to skip school and stay out after curfew, the JJS may directly and actively negate those parental wishes and require school attendance and observance of curfew laws. Juvenile laws defining dependent and neglected children place legal limits on the degree to which parents may allow their children freedom. Moreover, the moralistic message of the JJS clearly downgrades permissive parenting and complements strict parenting.

It seems quite inappropriate to allow the JJS to continue to support and even encourage strict and possibly oppressive parenting to the point of punishing children who do not comply with the strictest of parental rules. The JJS should not reenforce or encourage an extreme mode of parenting, either very strict or very permissive. The JJS should permit and encourage a wide range of parenting. Ways should be sought to provide children the legal means to refuse to comply with unreasonable parental demands and be free from harassment from parents or the JJS when they do so. Most assuredly, the JJS should not permit use of its resources and power to reenforce very restrictive and unrealistic parenting practices.

RECOMMENDATION 26: THE JJS SHOULD DEVELOP LAWS AND PROCEDURES TO SCREEN OUT ALLEGED ACTS OF DELINQUENCY RESULTING FROM CHILDREN'S NON-COMPLIANCE WITH UNREASONABLE PARENTAL DEMANDS.

One final unfortunate effect of the JJS is its tendency to give the crime-concerned public a false sense of security. Given the significant amount of serious crimes committed by children, the public understandably seeks protection. This results in a dependence upon the JJS by a public which is apparently ignorant of the general inability of the JJS to control juvenile crime.

The general public is apparently ignorant of facts well known to students of the JJS. These include such facts as that very few juvenile crimes are reported to the JJS, very few reported juvenile crimes result in identification of the perpetrator, very few identified perpetrators are adjudicated delinquent, and very few children adjudged delinquent avoid delinquent behavior in the future. Thus, the JJS can be a specific deterrent for only a very few children and has historically been quite ineffective even for those few. The general deterrence of the JJS is also highly suspect, given children's knowledge of its many weaknesses and loopholes. For the general public to rely upon such an impotent protector is a serious error.

The rhetoric of JJS agents and agencies is partly responsible for misleading the general public. Largely to justify their existence and to protect or increase their empires, JJS agents may loudly proclaim their determination to fight crime among children and change delinquent children into law-abiding citizens. The posture assumed by the police, prosecutors, judges, probation officers, and other JJS agents can tend to lull the general public into feeling that the "juvenile crime" problem is being taken care of by competent professionals who know what they are doing and will have the situation under control very soon. This is a great disservice to the public the JJS exists to serve. The JJS should be the primary provider of information about the ineffectiveness of the JJS in controlling delinquent behavior. The JJS should inform the general public that in a free and relatively uncontrolled society such as ours, social control through law is very difficult and affects very few actually delinquent children. Children can and regularly do commit serious acts of delinquency, and the nature of the JJS is such as to make almost all such acts untouchable by the JJS. If a child decides not to go to school, the JJS cannot prevent that act of delinquency short of assigning police escorts for all potential truants. If a child decides to burglarize a home, the chances of his being caught by the JJS are extremely low. The JJS tends to be a very coarse screen catching only those children who are extremely clumsy criminals or who come to the JJS and confess their activities.

The JJS has a responsibility to the general public to inform them as to the nature and extent of juvenile crime and the frank inability of the JJS in controlling juvenile crime. JJS agents need not be apologetic for this failure since it is due primarily to the nature of sociolegal control systems operating in a free society and to the personal morals and ethics of the citizens living in this society. Really effective control of juvenile crime will come about either when we have heavily armed police officers stationed at every possible site of juvenile crime or when our children avoid criminal behavior for reasons other than the threat of the JJS.

The JJS should be a strong proponent of discussion and research concerning the cause of delinquency and crime and extra-JJS means for preventing or reacting to delinquency and crime. The JJS should eagerly provide access to its records and activities for researchers and all persons interested in this problem. Any new ideas with any possibility of success should be encouraged and given a chance. The JJS should avoid seeking or accepting more funds and other support for JJS activities that have been ineffective for many years and show no real probability for effectiveness in the future. Ultimately the JJS should actively try to educate naive proponents of social control through expansion of the JJS. The JJS is in an ideal position to explain the very real limitations upon the social control abilities of any legal system, particularly the JJS. The JJS should encourage reduction in juvenile crime but should open their minds to other, more effective means of achieving this end.

RECOMMENDATION 27: THE JJS SHOULD EDUCATE THE GENERAL PUBLIC AS TO THE INABILITY OF THE JJS TO HAVE A SIGNIFICANT IMPACT ON JUVENILE CRIME AND SHOULD ACTIVELY SUPPORT DISCUSSION AND RESEARCH CONCERNING OTHER MEANS OF CHANGING THE BE-HAVIOR OF CHILDREN.

7. INFORMAL JJS

PROBLEMS AND RECOMMENDATIONS

In discussing the constitutionalized era of the formal JJS in chapter 2 above, the informal JJS was described as a collage of social service agencies serving the children of a community but not necessarily a regular part of the formal JJS. Analysis of the informal JJS would reveal almost exactly the same functions being performed as in the formal JJS but excluding the juvenile court judge, strict legal procedures, and formal juvenile court hearings. The misbehaving child is reported to an informal JJS agent, an investigation is conducted, a decision as to the child's misbehavior is made by an informal JJS agent, a "disposition" is designed for that child, and the "disposition" is administered by the informal JJS. Although the child is not formally adjudged to be a delinquent, the disposition imposed upon the child is typically quite similar to that which would have been imposed by the formal JJS. Such dispositions include counseling by a probation officer ("informal probation"), treatment by a psychologist or psychiatrist in a community mental health program, special tutoring for school, counseling and assistance for the entire family, and lodging in private closed institutions quite comparable in restrictions to state juvenile institutions (Morris, 1970).

While the formal JJS is composed primarily of police, prosecutors, defense attorneys, judges, probation officers, and institution counselors, the informal JJS is composed of school counselors, probation officers acting in an unofficial capacity, youth counselors from a variety of community agencies, and persons working within private institutions. The variety of community agencies differs widely according to the community, but typical agencies are youth service bureaus, youth crisis centers, drug counseling services, youth employment referral services, and similar agencies.

Many times one individual agency will constitute the entire informal JJS for a child. That is, the Youth Service Bureau (YSB) might be requested by a frustrated mother to intervene in her child's life, the YSB would investigate the situation and talk with the parents and child, a YSB agent would decide if the child was "guilty" and whether he needed "treatment," and, if so, design and impose a treatment program for that child and family. In this not-too-uncommon example, the YSB is functionally the entire informal JJS from initial report of the problem to enforcement of the disposition (Sherwood, 1972).

Three major problems will be discussed concerning the informal JJS. First is the relentless coercion for the child to participate "voluntarily" in the informal JJS; second, the unclear, inconsistent, and conflicting goals and operating principles of the informal JJS; third, the vast unchecked discretion now exercised by agents of the informal JJS.

First, consider the pressure on the apparently delinquent child to participate "voluntarily" in the informal JJS. For the child accused of an act of delinquency, the only alternative to "voluntary" cooperation with the informal JJS is being processed through the formal JJS (Croxton, 1967). In theory, the only coercing factor is the "threat" of "justice"; that is, to be processed by the formal JJS in a lawful and just manner and be dealt with as decided by the formal JJS. This alternative of formal JJS "justice" entails much more than is suggested by JJS rhetoric. We have considered previously the emotional impact of being apprehended by the police, transported to the police station in the back of a patrol car, and subjected to the dehumanizing records preparation process. The adjudicatory hearing and other preliminary hearings can be quite punitive in the emotional stress and conflict they visit upon a child. The last resort of the formal JJS—the state juvenile institution—will almost certainly cause irreparable harm to the child. This is the "justice" we threaten the child with in order to coerce him into "volunteering" for the informal JJS.

The coercion may begin early in the formal JJS. A school counselor may tell the child and his parents that unless he subjects himself to the informal JJS, the school counselor will have no choice but to report the child's delinquent acts to the police. A frustrated parent may threaten to call the police unless the child "volunteers" for the informal JJS. If the child is apprehended by the police, the juvenile police officer may suggest counseling by an informal JJS agency in lieu of formal referral of the case to juvenile court. The primary point of transfer to the informal JJS is the court screening juncture. The juvenile probation officer examines the case and may recommend informal or unofficial probation, with the alternative being the filing of a formal court petition alleging delinquency. At all these points the child can choose to "volunteer" for whatever informal counseling or other treatment program is being recommended and thus avoid any further punitive processing by the formal JJS.

It is readily apparent that the child typically does not have any effective means of avoiding the informal JJS. All the apparently knowledgeable adults are recommending the painless, attractive alternative as a favor to the child and working with him to avoid the harsh, punitive alternative. The child is told that the alternative to counseling is formal court action, and the ultimate punishment, the institution, is implied or even expressly threatened. It is critical to realize that the child has no defense attorney or neutral, objective, knowledgeable person from whom to seek advice. When the probation officer or police officer tells the child that he has ample evidence to send him to an institution, the child has no means of challenging that assertion or even making an educated guess as to that possibility. The child does not realize the extreme rarity of institutionalization, the dispositional characteristics of the current juvenile court judge, the predictable disposition for this kind of offense, etc. In short, the child is at the complete mercy of the informal JJS agent and has no source of objective and accurate information with which to make a decision.

The primary problem lies not with the intentions of or the service provided by the informal JJS agents and agencies. The problem is that this "voluntary" system for serving children in trouble is not in any meaningful way "voluntary." The solution lies not in doing away with or radically altering the informal JJS but in making its services available to children and families on a strictly voluntary basis without the present coercion. Making the system truly voluntary should increase the ability of the system to serve children since the children would participate because they sincerely wanted the services offered.

Several means exist for solving this problem. The formal JJS agents who shunt children off into the informal JJS can be required to eliminate their coercive techniques and simply inform children and their families of the availability of various services. The child's decision to seek such services would then have no effect on the decision to refer to court. The agents and agencies making up the informal JJS could saturate the community with information about the availability of their services and actively go out into the community to provide services to anyone asking for them. In order to provide an effective check on the over-zealous "child-helper," we could require that every child and family receive competent, personal legal advice as to the strength of the case against them and the probable outcome of the case if continued within the formal JJS. This legal advice would tend to offset the biased claims of police and probation officers as to the prosecutive merit of cases they have prepared themselves. The end result must be to continue to make available the present variety of services to children on an informal basis but to make them truly voluntary. Otherwise, we are subjecting children to JJS dispositions, either formal or informal, through threats and coercion without any realistic means for the child to avoid those dispositions.

> **RECOMMENDATION 28:** THE FORMAL AND INFORMAL JJSs SHOULD REENFORCE THE VOLUNTARY NATURE OF THE INFORMAL JJS BY REQUIRING FORMAL AND IN-FORMAL JJS AGENTS TO ADVISE ALL CHILDREN AND THEIR FAMILIES THAT ALL CHILDREN RECEIVE LEGAL ADVICE CONCERNING CASES AGAINST THEM, AND BY MINIMIZING THE EFFECT ON FORMAL JJS DECISIONS OF THE CHILD'S PARTICIPATION IN INFORMAL JJS ACTIVITIES.

A second major problem with the informal JJS is the unclear, inconsistent, and conflicting goals and operating principles of the various agencies within the informal JJS. The analysis of the formal JJS revealed many similar inconsistencies within a system that is much more cohesive and single-minded than the informal JJS. Although the formal JJS has no system manager, there are relatively few agencies to manage. Moreover, all the formal JJS agencies accept, or operate within, legal guidelines and requirements as established by *Gault* and its progeny. That is, the formal JJS is at least partly a legal system governed by and operating under law.

The informal JJS is not a legal system in any meaningful way, certainly not to the extent of the formal JJS. So long as the child and the family are "voluntarily" participating in a dispositional mode, few restrictions are placed upon agencies providing services. In fact, the informal JJS is made up of agencies with a wide variety of fundamental premises. One agency might be part of a fundamentalist Protestant church group and try to "save" all the children it counsels. Another agency might be staffed by local college students whose drug counseling concerning marijuana might be strikingly different from the drug counseling by the juvenile probation officer. A rural communal counseling agency might teach children that getting back to the land and leading a natural life is the only solution, while a neighborhood youth club teaches how to cope with life in the urban neighborhood. Confusion could well be the result for the child passed around from agency to agency and from counselor to counselor.

Conflicting goals and operating principles make evaluation of a child's "success" within the informal JJS almost impossible to measure meaningfully. Is the city teenager who doesn't get along well in the rural communal setting a failure? Is the child who accepts Jesus Christ as his personal Savior a success? Perhaps we must turn again to the effectiveness measure of reducing the frequency and/or seriousness of future acts of delinquency. Accuracy in this measurement is difficult enough in the formal JJS, in which the child is at least under some official supervision where repeated acts of delinquency will be somewhat difficult to hide. In the informal JJS the child is under very loose supervision if any, and often the "supervisors" are not official agents of the JJS who might feel an ethical duty to report all missteps by the child. The college student-drug counselor may be less willing to report to the police his counselee's admission of continued marijuana use than would be a probation officer for similar conduct of his probationer. The very informal, unofficial nature of the informal, unofficial JJS makes measurement of effectiveness most difficult if not impossible.

Even worse than the formal JJS's lack of a system manager is the lack of any meaningful supervision or coordination whatsoever for the informal JJS. Agencies which receive official referrals from the juvenile court or family court must meet various requirements and may be subject to inspection and evaluation, but no such requirements exist for the agencies of the informal JJS since no official referral is made. The children and their families are free to participate "voluntarily" in any activity which is not in itself illegal, regardless of the nature of the activity or the intrusion in the life of the child. While there might exist an "officially approved" list of informal youth service agencies, referrals to these agencies are typically made in private by individual JJS agents without any public hearing or even any record of what recommendation was made to the child by the agent. Thus, the appropriateness of the recommendation may be limited only by the recommender's particular faith in Jesus, Transcendental Meditation, team sports, or mountain climbing.

It is not recommended that this wide variety of community service agencies be prohibited from counseling children or be denied a right to exist. The problem lies with the present lack of any control over these agencies by the formal JJS. The formal JJS should continue to be aware of the services provided by these agencies and make this information available to all children in the community, including those of official interest to the JJS. However, the formal JJS should take measures to determine the goals and operating principles of these various agencies and not to recommend any agency which would not be utilized under a formal probation program. For example, specifically religious groups should be excluded because of First Amendment religious freedoms. Agencies presenting rather severe intrusions into a child's life should not be recommended, out of respect for the child's right to be left alone (McNulty, 1972-73). This is not to say that these agencies would be prohibited to children but simply that they would be excluded from the informal JJS at least as it is utilized by the formal JJS.

RECOMMENDATION 29: THE FORMAL AND INFORMAL JJSs SHOULD CLARIFY THE GOALS AND OPERATING PRINCIPLES OF ALL AGENCIES WORKING WITH CHILDREN AND THEIR FAMILIES IN ORDER TO ELIMINATE FROM THE INFORMAL JJS THOSE AGENCIES WHICH COULD NOT BE INCLUDED UNDER THE FORMAL JJS.

One last problem with the informal JJS is the vast, at times amazing, discretion exercised by informal JJS agents. The informal JJS is a personification of the rule of men, not of law, exactly the opposite of the fundamental premise of American sociolegal systems. In the informal JJS decisions are made almost totally by persons unsupervised in any meaningful way and unchecked by any systemic force. If the informal JJS agent decides that a certain child needs to participate in group counseling which involves intense personal attacks upon him by the group, that child must either participate in those group counseling sessions or be deemed a failure by that agent, by the agency, and typically by the informal JJS. Whether or not the group counseling was appropriate for that child and whether the group counseling was conducted in a reasonable manner are questions that may never be raised.

The socialized era of the formal JJS exhibited a similar kind of system for handling delinquent children. In that system the agents had almost total power over a child and could decide upon proper activities for the child without having their decisions effectively challenged. The bases for their decisions were almost never revealed and could be and were sometimes the most inappropriate factors. If a child's personal mannerisms were offensive to the agent, a rather severe sanction could be imposed without revealing the true reasons for that decision. *Gault* and numerous observers have soundly criticized unchecked discretion for decision makers with such awesome power over the lives of children. As a result, the socialized JJS was officially abolished and replaced by the constitutionalized or proceduralized JJS. JJS agents with such great powers over children were required to follow fairly rigid procedures, and their discretion was greatly reduced.

Regardless of *Gault*, the socialized JJS is alive and well and living within the informal JJS. The attitudes, prejudices, and discretionary practices which characterized the socialized JJS were simply moved over to the informal JJS to make room for the constitutionalized JJS. As a result of *Gault* and its progeny, the juvenile court judge can not escape constitutionalization and remains a captive within the new JJS. However, the role of the juvenile court judge from the socialized JJS was transported to the informal JJS and is now being played largely by the juvenile probation officer and occasionally by other youth counselors. Fitting the early descriptions of the juvenile court judge almost perfectly, the juvenile probation officer now is the person who may accept without challenge the truth of accusations against the child, examine the "whole child" including any personal characteristics the "judge" thinks important, and draw from his Solomon-like wisdom the proper course for the child to follow. As with the socialized JJS judge, this decision is effectively impossible to challenge without encountering a cure worse than the disease. No attorney represents the child's side of the case, no hearings are conducted, no particular procedures are followed, and no persuasive amount or kind of evidence must be produced. The child is simply accused of doing something authoritative adults find incorrect and is forced to accept often significant interference in his life, with the formal alternative being something all the apparently knowledgeable adults agree is much worse.

The child caught up in the informal JJS receives one particularly cruel punishment never imposed upon children caught up in the socialized JJS. In the socialized era children were never promised a fair hearing and a chance to challenge their accusers; they knew from the beginning that adults would decide their fate and they could but accept it. In the informal JJS children enter having been taught about justice for the accused and a right to their day in court, only to find that rhetoric to be without basis in reality.

The informal JJS must be proceduralized much as was the socialized JJS. Decisions having significant impact upon children and their families must be subject to review by objective persons and according to objective, nondiscriminatory principles. For the same reasons we protect children from the socialized JJS, we must proceduralize the informal JJS. Of course, history tells us that as soon as we proceduralize the informal JJS a third, parallel JJS will emerge to divert children again away from both proceduralized JJSs and process them in a discretionary manner. It seems that persons who work with troubled children refuse actually to give up their discretionary power over children and if denied overt exercise of that power in one dimension will simply find another dimension in which to act. When we took away vast discretion from the judge, the discretion seemed to migrate to the probation officer. If we take it away from the probation officer, will the juvenile police officer become the new "judge," or will it be the school counselor or another agent as yet unknown to the JJS? The very nature of the JJS agents is apparently to do what they think best for children under their control and to find inventive ways to accomplish this end in spite of laws, regulations, job descriptions, etc. The only solution, albeit a most regretful one, is to remove as much discretion as possible from all JJS agents. This was recommended previously for agents within the formal JJS and must also be recommended for agents within the informal JJS. As was persuasively explained in *Gault,* following proper procedures need not prevent agents and agencies from serving the needs of children. These agents and agencies should simply reveal the bases for their decisions, subject those decisions to the scrutiny of supervisors and others, and impose only minimum-intervention treatment programs upon children.

RECOMMENDATION 30: THE FORMAL AND INFORMAL JJSs SHOULD ACT TO REDUCE TO A MINIMUM THE UNCHECKED DISCRETION EXERCISED BY AGENTS OF THE INFORMAL JJS OVER THE LIVES OF CHILDREN REFERRED TO THEM BY THE FORMAL JJS.

8. CONCLUSION

The foregoing JJS functional analysis and thirty (plus one) recommendations for change reveal the JJS as it is now and as it could be. The JJS is in need of immediate attention to specific problems which can be alleviated without major revisions and within limits acceptable to the general public. For example, relatively little change is involved in limiting the roles of police and probation officers and increasing the roles of prosecutors and defense attorneys. Other, more fundamental and systemic problems are deserving of further study. Obviously, such goals as avoiding perpetuation of class hatreds will be difficult to achieve.

One area needing immediate attention is the role of police within the JJS. Police should be much less involved in the JJS, ideally being used only to apprehend and detain dangerously violent children. The specter of police apprehending (arresting), preparing records concerning (booking), and detaining (jailing) children for such dangerously violent acts as skipping class, running away, and disobeying oppressive parents is a gross misuse of JJS personnel, funds, and efforts. The harmful effects of the JJS for those children are incalculable. Police action is justifiable only for the protection of society from children who cause injury to people and damage to property. The present JJS allows use of police as would the frustrated mother who threatens her child with "Wait until your father gets home!" JJS punishment of children through unnecessary police action is a serious problem which could be simply solved: prohibit any official police contact with suspected delinquent children unless absolutely necessary to quell violent action.

Lawyers—both prosecutors and respondents' attorneys—should be more involved in the JJS. Prosecuting attorneys are desperately needed on a regular, full-time basis. The petitioner, parents, probation officers, and other JJS agents regularly have a critical need for legal advice concerning JJS activities. The prosecuting attorney must accept responsibility for evaluating the prosecutive merit of a case, engage in response negotiations, and present evidence in court. The lack of significant participation by prosecuting attorneys in most JJSs is one of the most serious flaws in the present JJS. Defense attorneys, or more properly "respondents' attorneys," are also utilized in insufficient quantity within the formal and informal JJSs. Legal advice is particularly unavailable for children threatened by or caught up in the informal JJS.

The other JJS lawyer—the juvenile court judge—should be more than a lawyer. We must develop requirements for juvenile court judges which combine the best from the socialized and constitutionalized JJSs. We should retain the procedurally expert judge required by the post-*Gault* JJS, but should also retain the socially expert judge from the pre-*Gault* JJS. *Gault* does not require that juvenile court judges be lawyers only; it should be read as adding the requirement of legal expertise to the ideal model of the socialized JJS judge.

JJS probation officers have, through unchecked discretion, literally taken over the JJS and presently exercise awesome power over children's lives. No one person should have such power. Probation officers' discretion should be markedly reduced; they should be required to follow fairly explicit guidelines and to explain in writing the bases for their decisions. One probation officer should not be allowed to handle the same case for several years through all stages of several charges. Probation officers, like the rest of us, are susceptible to allowing personal frustration and rejection to affect their professional decisions. Probation officers must be protected from this tendency, and children must be protected from probation officers.

JJS agents in juvenile institutions should recognize the unavoidable harm to children inflicted by such institutions. Children should be made clearly aware of this harm, and intensive efforts should be made to counteract this harm. While we have developed no reasonable alternative to incarceration for some children, we have an obligation to incarcerated children to minimize the harm inflicted upon them.

Juvenile institutions, as well as juvenile probation programs, should concentrate upon teaching older children the various adult techniques for coping with the world as it exists. Training older delinquent children for proper behavior in a child role they will never again play is of little value. JJS corrections counselors must analyze the reality of their counselees, now and in the future, and counsel accordingly.

Analysis of the JJS also reveals more fundamental, systemic problems.

One is the pervasive "right to custody" theme. This fundamental premise is the basis for denying freedom of action and behavior for children. The infant's human right to be cared for has been extrapolated to include the incarceration of teenagers for noncriminal and nonthreatening behavior. This problem is fundamental since the right to custody is a major part of the foundation of the JJS, which assumes that the JJS can and does provide proper parental care. It is this fundamental premise that is relied upon by police to apprehend and detain children and by juvenile courts to order incarceration of children in institutions. The JJS should abandon the right to custody and admit that governmental custody does not and probably can never approximate proper parental care.

Another fundamental problem is that the JJS is a sociolegal system designed and operated to produce achievements beyond the realm of modern knowledge. It is comparable to a vast public health system designed and operated to deliver the cure for cancer to all citizens in spite of the fact that the cure for cancer is unknown at this time. The JJS is asked to deliver the "cure" for juvenile delinquency even though such a "cure" is presently unknown. Not unlike the cancer system, the JJS delivers many "potions" which mask symptoms and temporarily satisfy society's demand for action. After eighty years of discouraging failure by the JJS, matched with hundreds of years of comparable failure by the CJS, our society should face this reality and actively support research and carefully controlled experimentation concerning other means of changing and controlling the behavior of children.

Unchecked discretion in all aspects of the JJS is another fundamental problem. Major sources of unfair treatment and counterproductive decisions are police discretion to refer to court, probation officer discretion to file a court petition or cause diversion to the informal JJS, and institution officer discretion to release on or revoke parole. While a cursory analysis would seem to justify ample discretion for well-educated and experienced professionals, practice has shown that such discretion too often results in the use of the JJS as a means of enforcing personal prejudices and values. In *Gault* the Court deemed it necessary to curtail greatly the unchecked discretion of the juvenile court judge. The same must now be done concerning all other agents of the formal and informal JJSs.

The JJS also provides official sanction for unfair public discrimination against children as a minority group within society. Corollary to this is the tendency to split children into classes, pitting favored, unlabeled children against delinquent children. The result is to deny many basic human rights to children simply on the basis of age, as well as to instill class hatreds in children. This is not a simple flaw in design or an operational problem to be corrected; this is fundamental to the existence of the JJS. While these effects can be reduced significantly by careful pruning, the essential effect is unavoidable as long as the JJS exists. One final conclusion must be suggested. Although we know in some detail how the JJS is designed and operated, we have little reason to believe that the JJS causes less juvenile delinquency than would otherwise exist. We do know that juvenile delinquency as defined by juvenile laws is pervasive in our society and that modifications in the JJS seem to have little correlation with the amount or nature of juvenile delinquency. In contrast, it is clear that the JJS causes much future juvenile delinquency and adult crime by the experiences it provides for children.

Society must ask whether the beneficial effects of the JJS are worth the costs to society and its children. Such a question requires freedom from centuries-old assumptions about law and deviance. Such a question implies that law—particularly juvenile law—has provided little control of dangerous deviance and certainly has not produced a peaceful and relatively crime-free society. Satisfactory answers to this question should not be sought solely from tedious manipulation of the JJS. We must look outside of and beyond the JJS for control of dangerous deviance by our children.

BIBLIOGRAPHY

Alers, Miriam G. 1973. "Transfer of Jurisdiction from Juvenile to Criminal Court." *Crime and Delinquency* 19: 519-27.

Allman, Robert L., III. 1972. "Admissibility of Juvenile Confessions: Is an Intelligent and Knowing Waiver of Constitutional Rights Possible without Adult Guidance?" *University of Pittsburgh Law Review* 34: 321-28.

"The Applicability of the Fourth Amendment Exclusionary Rule to Juveniles in Delinquency Proceedings." 1972. *Columbia Human Rights Law Review* 4: 417-49.

Ariessohn, Richard M., and Frederick I. Closson. 1971. "Alternatives to Juvenile Detention." *California Youth Authority Quarterly* 24: 17-26.

Arnold, William R. 1970. *Juveniles on Parole: A Sociological Perspective.* New York: Random House.

Arthur, Lindsey G. 1970. "Disposition: The Forgotten Focus." *Juvenile Court Judge's Journal* 21 (3): 71-73.

Austin, Kenneth M., and Fred R. Speidel. 1971. "Thunder: An Alternative to Juvenile Court Appearance." *California Youth Authority Quarterly* 24: 13-16.

Bazelon, David L. 1969. "The Right to Treatment: A Symposium." *Georgetown Law Journal* 57: 676-79.

Berenson, Harvey. 1969. "The Lawyer in Juvenile Court." *Journal of the Kansas Bar Association* 38: 15-18, 60-64.

Besharov, Douglas J. 1974. *Juvenile Justice Advocacy: Practice in a Unique Court.* New York: Practicing Law Institute.

Blank, Robert H. 1972. "Constitutional Law: The Jury and the Juvenile Court." *University of Florida Law Review* 24: 385-92.

Blinick, Michael. 1968. "Delinquency and Justice." *Catholic Lawyer* 14: 233-45.

Bottoms, A. E., and F. H. McClintock. 1974. *Criminals Coming of Age: A Study of Institutional Adaptation in the Treatment of Adolescent Offenders.* New York: Humanities Press.

Brennan, William C. 1970. "The Probation Officer's Perception of the Attorney's Role in Juvenile Court." *Crime and Delinquency Quarterly* 16: 172-80.

Brennan, William C., and S. K. Klinduka. 1970. "Role Expectations of Social Workers and Lawyers in Juvenile Court." *Crime and Delinquency Quarterly* 16: 191-201.

Brusten, M. 1972. "Criminalization Caused by Social Agencies: An Analysis of Child Welfare Office Records." *Neue Praxis* 1: 174-89.

Burd, Lee R. 1970. "Waiver of Jurisdiction in the Juvenile Court: Another *Gault* Question Still Unanswered." *South Dakota Law Review* 15: 376–85.

Caldwell, Robert G. 1966. "The Juvenile Court: Its Development and Some Major Problems," in Rose Giallombardo (ed.), *Juvenile Delinquency: A Book of Readings*. New York: John Wiley and Sons.

Chase, Edward. 1974. "Questioning the Juvenile Commitment: Some Notes on Method and Consequence." *Indiana Law Review* 8 (2): 373–93.

———. 1973. "Schemes and Visions: A Suggested Revision of Juvenile Sentencing." *Texas Law Review* 51: 673–706.

Cicourel, Aaron V. 1968. *The Social Organization of Juvenile Justice.* New York: John Wiley and Sons.

Clark, Betty J. 1972. "Do Juvenile Courts Have a Duty to Supervise Child Care Agencies and Juvenile Detention Facilities?" *Harvard Law Journal* 17: 443–55.

Clemens, Cameron L. 1969. "Continuity through a Lasting Parentship." *Public Welfare* 27 (4): 338–43.

Coffey, Alan R. 1974. *Juvenile Justice As a System: Law Enforcement to Rehabilitation.* Englewood Cliffs, N. J.: Prentice-Hall.

Cogan, Neil H. 1970. "Juvenile Law before and after the Entrance of 'Parens Patriae.'" *South Carolina Law Review* 22: 147–81.

Cole, Larry, 1972. *Our Children's Keepers: Inside America's Kid Prisons.* New York: Grossman Publishers.

Commonwealth v. Fisher, 213 Pa. St. 48, 62 A.198 (1905).

Cooley, Thomas M. 1971. "Court Control over Treatment of Juvenile Offenders." *Duquesne Law Review* 9: 613–25.

"Crime's Big Payoff." 1976. *U. S. News and World Report* 70 (6): 50–52.

Croxton, Tom A. 1967. "The Juvenile Court: Some Current Issues." *Child Welfare* 46: 553–61.

Culbertson, Robert G. 1973. "Commitment Practices in Indiana's Juvenile Courts." *Juvenile Justice* 24 (3): 25–30.

Davis, Samuel M. 1971. "Justice for the Juvenile: The Decision to Arrest and Due Process." *Duke Law Journal* 1971: 913–37.

———. 1974. *Rights of Juveniles: The Juvenile Justice System.* New York: Clark Boardman Company.

"The Dilemma of the 'Uniquely Juvenile' Offender." 1972. *William and Mary Law Review* 14: 386–408.

Drinan, Robert F. 1969. "Aftermath of Apprehension: Family Lawyer's Response." *Prospectus: A Journal of Law Reform* 3: 31–38.

Duffee, David, and Larry Siegel. 1971. "The Organization Man: Legal Counsel in the Juvenile Court." *Criminal Law Bulletin* 7: 544–53.

Dyson, Elizabeth D., and Richard B. Dyson. 1968. "Family Courts in the United States, Parts I and II." *Journal of Family Law* 8: 505–86.

Edwards, James L. 1971. "In Loco Parentis: Definitions, Application and Implication." *South Carolina Law Review* 23: 114–26.

Eldefonso, Edward. 1973. *Law Enforcement and the Youthful Offender: Juvenile Procedures.* Second edition. New York: John Wiley and Sons.

———. 1972. *Youth Problems and Law Enforcement.* Englewood Cliffs, N. J.: Prentice-Hall.

Eldefonso, Edward, and Alan R. Coffey. 1976. *Process and Impact of the Juvenile Justice System.* Beverly Hills, Cal.: Glencoe Press.

Eldefonso, Edward, and Walter Hartinger. 1976. *Control, Treatment, and Rehabilitation of Juvenile Offenders.* Beverly Hills, Cal.: Glencoe Press.

Equi, Glenn C., et al. 1967. "*In Re Gault:* Understanding the Attorney's New Role." *Villanova Law Review* 12: 803–38.

Erickson, Patricia G. 1974. "The Defense Lawyer's Role in Juvenile Court: An Empirical Investigation into Judges' and Social Workers' Points of View." *University of Toronto Law Journal* 24: 126–48.

"Facts and Law of Inter-Institutional Transfer of Juveniles." 1968. *Maine Law Review* 20: 93-141.

Fairlie, Chester. 1972. "Appellate Review of Juvenile Court Dispositions: *Gault's* Forgotten Footnote." *Connecticut Law Review* 5: 117-42.

Fant, Fred D. 1969. "Impact of the Gault Decision on Probation Practices in Juvenile Court." *Federal Probation* 33: 14-18.

Faust, Frederic L., and Paul J. Brantingham (eds.). 1974. *Juvenile Justice Philosophy: Readings, Cases and Comments.* St. Paul: West Publishing Company.

Ferdinand, Theodore N., and Elmer G. Luchterband. 1970. "Inner-City Youths, the Police, the Juvenile Courts, and Justice." *Social Problems* 17: 510-27.

Ferster, Elyce Z., and Thomas F. Courtless. 1969. "The Beginnings of Juvenile Justice, Police Practices, and the Juvenile Offender." *Vanderbilt Law Review* 22: 567-608.

———. 1971. "Intake Process in the Affluent County Juvenile Court." *Hastings Law Journal* 22: 1127-53.

———. 1972a. "Post-Dispositional Treatment and Recidivism in the Juvenile Court: Towards Justice for All." *Journal of Family Law* 11: 683-709.

———. 1972b. "Pre-Dispositional Data, Role of Counsel and Decisions in a Juvenile Court." *Law and Society Review* 7: 195-222.

Ferster, Elyce Z., Thomas F. Courtless, and Edith N. Snethen. 1970. "Separating Official and Unofficial Delinquents: Juvenile Court Intake." *Iowa Law Review* 55: 864-93.

Ferster, Elyce Z., et al. 1969. "Juvenile Detention: Protection, Prevention of Punishment?" *Fordham Law Review* 38: 161-96.

Flammang, C. J. 1972. *Police Juvenile Enforcement.* Springfield, Ill.: Charles C. Thomas, Publisher.

———. 1973. "Reflections on the Police Juvenile Enterprise." *Juvenile Justice* 24 (1): 22-27.

Forer, Lois G. 1970. *"No One Will Lissen": How Our Legal System Brutalizes the Youthful Poor.* New York: Grosset & Dunlap.

Fox, Sanford J. 1972. *Cases and Materials on Modern Juvenile Justice.* St. Paul: West Publishing Company.

———. 1970. "Juvenile Justice Reform: An Historical Perspective." *Stanford Law Review* 22: 1187-1239.

———. 1971. *The Law of Juvenile Courts in a Nutshell.* St. Paul: West Publishing Company.

Frey, Martin A., and Charles P. Bubany. 1972-73. "Pre-Adjudication Review of the Social Record in Juvenile Court: A Low-Visibility Obstacle to a Fair Process." *Journal of Family Law* 12: 391-404.

Gallegos v. State of Colorado, 370 U.S. 49 (1962).

Garabedian, Peter G., and Don C. Gibbons. 1971. *Becoming Delinquent: Young Offenders and the Correctional System.* Chicago: Aldine Publishing Company.

Garner, M. Craig, Jr. 1973. "Due Process and Waiver of Juvenile Court Jurisdiction." *Washington and Lee Law Review* 30: 591-613.

Gold, Martin, and Jay R. Williams. 1969. "National Study of the Aftermath of Apprehension." *Prospectus: A Journal of Law Reform* 3: 3-12.

Gough, Aidan R. 1971a. "The Beyond-Control Child and the Right to Treatment: An Exercise in the Synthesis of Paradox." *St. Louis University Law Journal* 16: 182-200.

———. 1971b. "Consent Decrees and Informal Services in the Juvenile Court: Excursions toward Balance." *University of Kansas Law Review* 19: 733-46.

Greenberg, William G. 1972. "The Consent Decree and the New York Family Court Procedure in 'JD' and 'PINS' Cases." *Syracuse Law Review* 23: 1211-25.

Greenspan, Julian. 1969. "Role of the Attorney in Juvenile Court." *Cleveland-Marshall Law Review—Cleveland State Law Review* 18: 599-609.

Hahn, Paul H. 1971. *The Juvenile Offender and the Law.* Cincinnati: W. H. Anderson Company.

Haley v. State of Ohio, 332 U.S. 596 (1948).

Hammergren, Donald R. 1973. "The Role of Juvenile Detention in a Changing Juvenile Justice System." *Juvenile Justice* 24 (3): 46–49.

Hausman, Anne K. 1972. "The Administrative Transfer of Juveniles from Juvenile to Adult Penal Institutions." *St. Louis University Law Journal* 16: 479–96.

Horowitz, Allan H., and Nancy L. Nickerson. 1972. *"McKeiver v. Pennsylvania:* A Retreat in Juvenile Justice." *Brooklyn Law Review* 38: 650–92.

Hussey, Frederick A. 1976. "Perspectives on Parole Decision-Making with Juveniles." *Criminology* 13 (4): 449–69.

Hynes, Christian, 1972. "Principles Governing Intake in Children's Institutions." *Federal Probation* 36: 27–29.

In Re Gault, 387 U.S. 1, 87 S. Ct. 1428, 18 L. Ed. 2d 527 (1967).

In Re Winship, 397 U.S. 358, 90 S. Ct. 1068, 25 L. Ed. 2d 368 (1970).

Ismael, James D., Jr. 1972. "Juvenile Right to Counsel at Probation Revocation Hearing." *Journal of Family Law* 11: 745–52.

James, Howard. 1971. *Children in Trouble: A National Scandal.* New York: David McKay Company.

Johnson, Thomas A. 1975. *Introduction to the Juvenile Justice System.* St. Paul: West Publishing Company.

"Juvenile Courts: Juveniles in Delinquency Proceedings Are Not Constitutionally Entitled to the Right of Trial by Jury—*McKeiver v. Pennsylvania.*" 1972. *Michigan Law Review* 70: 171–94.

"Juvenile Delinquency: Procedural Requirements in Disciplinary Proceedings within Juvenile Institutions." 1967. *Boston University Law Review* 52: 480–93.

"Juvenile Delinquents: The Police, State Courts, and Individualized Justice." 1966. *Harvard Law Review* 79: 775–810.

"Juvenile Police Record-Keeping." 1972. *Columbia Human Rights Law Review* 4: 462–84.

Kalnins, John M. 1971. "Right to Bail for Juveniles." *Chicago-Kent Law Review* 48: 99–106.

Kapner, Lewis. 1973. "The Juveniles' Right to Treatment: The Next Step." *Florida Bar Journal* 47: 228–31.

Kay, Richard, and Daniel Segal. 1973. "Role of the Attorney in Juvenile Court Process: A Non-Polar Approach." *Georgetown Law Journal* 61: 1401–24.

Kent v. United States, 383 U.S. 541, 86 S. Ct. 1045, 16 L. Ed. 2d 84 (1966).

Ketcham, Orman W., and Monrad G. Paulsen. 1967. *Cases and Materials Relating to Juvenile Courts.* Brooklyn: Foundation Press.

Kittrie, Nicholas N. 1969. "Can the Right to Treatment Remedy the Ills of the Juvenile Process?" *Georgetown Law Journal* 57: 848–85.

–––. 1971. *The Right to be Different: Deviance and Enforced Therapy.* Baltimore: Penguin Books.

Klaber, Jane K. 1973. "Person in Need of Supervision: Is There a Constitutional Right to Treatment?" *Brooklyn Law Review* 39: 624–57.

Klapmutz, Nora. 1972. "Children's Rights: The Legal Rights of Minors in Conflict with Law or Social Custom." *Crime and Delinquency Literature* 4 (3): 449–77.

Klein, Malcolm M., Susan L. Rosenzweig, and Ronald Bates. 1975. "The Ambiguous Juvenile Arrest." *Criminology* 13 (1): 78–89.

Kobetz, Richard W. 1971. *The Police Role and Juvenile Delinquency.* Gaithersburg, Md.: International Association of Chiefs of Police.

Kobetz, Richard W., and Betty B. Bosarge. 1973. *Juvenile Justice Administration.* Gaithersburg, Md.: International Association of Chiefs of Police.

Kratcoski, P. C., and F. Hernandez. 1974. "Application of Management Principles to the Juvenile Justice System." *Juvenile Justice* 25: 39–44.

Langley, Michael H. 1972. "The Juvenile Court: The Making of a Delinquent." *Law and Society Review* 7: 273–98.

Law Enforcement Assistance Administration. 1971. *Planning and Designing for Juvenile Justice*. Washington: Law Enforcement Assistance Administration, 1971.

Lefstein, Norman, Vaughan Stapleton, and Lee Teitelbaum. 1969. "In Search of Juvenile Justice: *Gault* and Its Implementation." *Law and Society Review* 3: 491-562.

Littleton, Martin W. 1966. *Opening to the Court or Jury*. New York: Practicing Law Institute.

Lockwood, Robert W. 1968. "The Role of the Attorney in the Treatment Phase of the Juvenile Court Process." *St. Louis University Law Journal* 12: 659-78.

Loftquist, William A. 1967. "The Framework and Experience of Juvenile Probation." *Social Casework* 48: 17-21.

McCarty, William M. 1973. "Juvenile Justice: The Economics of Ineptitude." *San Diego Law Review* 10: 250-65.

McGuire, Joan M. 1973. "Discovery Rights in Juvenile Proceedings." *University of San Francisco Law Review* 7: 333-47.

McHardy, Louis W. 1973. "Assessment of Juvenile Probation Services." *Juvenile Justice* 24 (2): 41-46.

Mack, Julian W. 1909. "The Juvenile Court." *Harvard Law Review* 23: 104-22.

McKeiver v. Pennsylvania, 403 U.S. 528, 91 S. Ct. 1976, 29 L. Ed. 2d 647 (1971).

McLean, Gordon R. 1969. *We're Holding Your Son*. Old Tappan, N.J.: Fleming H. Revell Company.

McNulty, Jill K. 1972-73. "The Right to Be Left Alone." *Journal of Family Law* 12: 229-55.

Mennel, Robert M. 1972. "Origins of the Juvenile Court: Changing Perspectives on the Legal Rights of Juvenile Delinquents." *Crime and Delinquency* 18: 68-78.

Merz, Charles L. 1968. "Representing the Juvenile Defendant in Waiver Proceedings." *St. Louis University Law Journal* 12: 424-65.

Midoneck, Millard L., and Douglas J. Besharov. 1972. *Children, Parents, and the Courts: Juvenile Delinquency, Ungovernability, and Neglect*. New York: Practicing Law Institute.

Miller, Frank W., Robert O. Dawson, George E. Dix, and Raymond I. Parnas. 1971. *The Juvenile Justice Process*. Mineola, N.Y.: Foundation Press.

Mora, Steven H. 1969. "Juvenile Detention: A Constitutional Problem Affecting Local Government." *Urban Lawyer* 1: 189-216.

Morris, Joe A. 1970. *First Offender: A Volunteer Program for Youth in Trouble with the Law*. New York: Funk and Wagnalls.

Murphy, Patrick T. 1969. "Defending a Juvenile Court Proceeding." *Practical Lawyer* 15: 31-40.

———. 1974. *Our Kindly Parent—The State: The Juvenile Justice System and How It Works*. New York: Viking Press.

Newman, Charles L. 1968. "The Constructive Use of Police Authority with Youth and Families in Crisis." *Police* 12: 18-23.

O'Donnell, Kevin M. 1972. "Inferential Impeachment: The Presence of Parole Officers at Subsequent Juvenile Adjudications." *Marquette Law Review* 55: 349-68.

O'Rourke, Thomas P., and Richard G. Salem. 1968. "A Comparative Analysis of Pretrial Release Procedures." *Crime and Delinquency* 14: 367-73.

Palmier, Joseph R. 1968. "Juvenile Court Intake: Form and Function." *Willamette Law Journal* 5: 121-30.

Peterson, R. Thomas. 1972. "Juvenile Justice and Pre-Adjudication Detentions." *UCLA-Alaska Law Review* 1: 154-71.

Pirsig, Maynard E. 1969. "The Constitutional Validity of Confining Disruptive Delinquents in Penal Institutions." *Minnesota Law Review* 54: 101-45.

Platt, Anthony M. 1969. *The Child Savers: The Invention of Delinquency*. Chicago: University of Chicago Press.

Popkin, Alice, and Freda Lippert. 1971. "Is There a Constitutional Right to the Insanity Defense in Juvenile Court?" *Journal of Family Law* 10: 421–42.

Portune, Robert. 1971. *Changing Adolescent Attitudes towards Police.* Cincinnati: W. H. Anderson Company.

President's Commission on Law Enforcement and Administration. 1967. *The Challenge of Crime in a Free Society.* Washington: U.S. Government Printing Office.

Pursuit, Dan G. 1972. *Police Programs for Preventing Crime and Delinquency.* Springfield, Ill.: Charles C. Thomas, Publisher.

Pyfer, John F., Jr. 1972. "The Juvenile's Right to Receive Treatment." *Family Law Quarterly* 6: 279–320.

Ralston, William H., Jr. 1971. "Intake: Informal Disposition or Adversary Proceeding?" *Crime and Delinquency* 17: 160–67.

Ramo, Simon. 1969. *Cure for Chaos: Fresh Solutions to Social Problems through the Systems Approach.* New York: David McKay Company.

Reinhold, Robert J. 1968. "The Role of the Attorney in Juvenile Court Intake Processes." *St. Louis University Law Journal* 13: 69–89.

Rendleman, Douglas R. 1971. "Parens Patriae: From Chancery to the Juvenile Court." *South Carolina Law Review* 23: 205–59.

Renn, Donna A. 1973. "The Right to Treatment and the Juvenile." *Crime and Delinquency* 19: 477–84.

Ritter, Robert F. 1968. "The Role of the Lawyer in Preparation for a Delinquency Hearing in Juvenile Court." *St. Louis University Law Journal* 12: 631–43.

Rogers, Kristine O. 1972. ""For Her Own Protection . . .": Conditions of Incarceration for Female Juvenile Offenders in the State of Connecticut." *Law and Society Review* 7: 223–46.

Ruppert, Ernest R. 1971–72. "Juvenile Criminal Proceedings in Federal Courts." *Loyola Law Review* 18: 133–49.

Sanders, Wiley B. 1945: "Some Early Beginnings of the Children's Court Movement in England." *National Probation Association Yearbook:* New York: National Council on Crime and Delinquency.

Sanders, Wiley B. (ed.) 1970. *Juvenile Offenders for a Thousand Years: Selected Readings from Anglo-Saxon Times to 1900.* Chapel Hill: University of North Carolina Press.

Sarosiek, Peter A. 1973. "Constitutional Law—Due Process: Revocation of a Juvenile's Parole." *Wisconsin Law Review* 3: 954–62.

Sarri, R. C. 1973. "Detention of Youth in Jails and Juvenile Detention Facilities." *Juvenile Justice* 24: 2–18.

Saylor, Charles H. 1973. "Interrogation of Juveniles: The Right to a Parent's Presence." *Dickinson Law Review* 77: 543–60.

Scarpitt, Frank R., and Richard M. Stephenson. 1971. "Juvenile Court Dispositions: Factors in the Decision-Making Process." *Crime and Delinquency* 17: 142–51.

Schornhorst, F. Thomas. 1968. "The Waiver of Juvenile Court Jurisdiction: *Kent* Revisited." *Indiana Law Journal* 43: 583–613.

Schultz, J. Lawrence. 1973. "The Cycle of Juvenile Court History." *Crime and Delinquency* 19: 457–76.

Schultz, Leroy G. 1967. "The Pre-Sentence Investigation and Victimology." *University of Missouri at Kansas City Law Review* 35: 247–60.

Schur, Edwin M. 1971. *Labeling Deviant Behavior: Its Sociological Implications.* New York: Harper and Row.

———. 1973. *Radical Nonintervention: Rethinking the Delinquency Problem.* Englewood Cliffs, N. J.: Prentice-Hall.

Schwarzenberger, Susan. 1971. "Juvenile Probation: Restrictions, Rights and Rehabilitation." *St. Louis University Law Journal* 16: 276–93.

Scott, Joseph W., and Jerry B. Hissong. 1969. "Changing the Delinquent Subculture: A Sociological Approach." *Crime and Delinquency* 15: 449–509.

Sheridan, William H. 1968. "The Gault Decision and the Probation Services." *Indiana Law Journal* 43: 655–60.

Sherman, Peter R. 1968. "'. . . Nor Cruel and Unusual Punishments Inflicted': The Eighth Amendment and the Juvenile Court." *Crime and Delinquency* 14: 73–84.

Sherwood, Norman. 1972. *The Youth Service Bureau: A Key to Delinquency Prevention.* Paramus, N. J.: National Council on Crime and Delinquency.

Shoben, Elaine W. 1973. "The Interrogated Juvenile: Caveat Confessor?" *Hastings Law Journal* 24: 413–30.

Shullenberger, J. D., and P. T. Murphy. 1973. "Crisis in Juvenile Courts: Is Bifurcation an Answer?" *Chicago Bar Record* 55: 117–84.

Simms, Larry L. 1972. "Courts, the Constitution, and Juvenile Institutional Reform." *Boston University Law Review* 52: 33–63.

Skoler, Daniel J. 1968. "Counsel in Juvenile Court Proceedings: A Total Criminal Justice Perspective." *Journal of Family Law* 8: 243–77.

Smith, James H. 1971. "Juvenile Right to Bail." *Journal of Family Law* 11: 81–105.

Snyder, Eloise C. 1971. "Impact of the Juvenile Court Hearing on the Child." *Crime and Delinquency* 17: 180–90.

Somerville, James G. 1969. "A Study of the Preventive Aspect of Police Work with Juveniles." *Criminal Law Review* 1969: 407–14, 472–84.

Stapleton, William V., and Lee Teitelbaum. 1972. *In Defense of Youth: A Study of the Role of Counsel in American Juvenile Courts.* New York: Russell Sage Foundation.

Statton, J. 1974. "Crisis Intervention Counseling and Police Diversion from the Juvenile Justice System: A Review of the Literature." *Juvenile Justice* 25: 44–53.

Steketee, John P. 1969. "Aftermath of Apprehension: Juvenile Court Judge's Response." *Prospectus: A Journal of Law Reform* 3: 25–30.

Streib, Victor L. 1973. *Study Guide for P475: American Juvenile Justice System.* Bloomington: Indiana University Division of Continuing Education.

Sumner, Helen. 1971. "Locking Them Up." *Crime and Delinquency* 17: 168–79.

Sundeen, Richard A., Jr. 1972. *A Study of Factors Related to Police Diversion of Juveniles: Departmental Policy and Structure, Community Attachment, and Professionalization of Police.* Dissertation. Ann Arbor: University Microfilms.

Teitelbaum, Lee. 1967. "The Use of Social Reports in Juvenile Court Adjudications." *Journal of Family Law* 7: 425–41.

Tenney, Charles W. 1969. "The Utopian World of the Juvenile Courts." *Annals of the American Academy of Political and Social Sciences* 383: 101–18.

Terry, Robert M. 1967. "The Screening of Juvenile Offenders." *Journal of Criminal Law, Criminology and Police Science* 58: 173–81.

Thomas, Charles W., and Christopher M. Sieverdes. 1975. "Juvenile Court Intake: An Analysis of Discretionary Decision-Making." *Criminology* 12(4): 413–32.

Thomas, Mason P., Jr. 1971. *Juvenile Corrections: Five Issues To Be Faced.* Washington: United States Government Printing Office.

Thornberry, Terrence P. 1973. "Race, Socio-Economic Status and Sentencing in the Juvenile Justice System." *Journal of Criminal Law and Criminology* 64 (1): 90–98.

Trojanowicz, Robert C. 1973. *Juvenile Delinquency: Concepts and Control.* Englewood Cliffs, N. J.: Prentice-Hall.

Vandiver, James V. 1970. "Juvenile Records Are Justifiable." *Police* 15: 41–42.

Virijevich, Diane. 1976. Master's thesis. Department of Forensic Studies, Indiana University, Bloomington.

Walsh, Joseph T. 1968. "The Attorney and the Dispositional Process: Attorney's Role in Formal Dispositions." *St. Louis University Law Journal* 12: 644–58.

Walters, David R. 1975. *Physical and Sexual Abuse of Children: Causes and Treatment.* Bloomington: Indiana University Press.

Waterman, Nairn. 1970. "Disclosure of Social and Psychological Reports at Disposition." *Osgoode Hall Law Journal* 7: 213–33.

Weiner, Norman L., and Charles V. Willie. 1971. "Decisions by Juvenile Officers." *American Journal of Sociology* 77: 199–210.

Wenk, E. A., and R. L. Emrich. 1972. "Assaultive Youth: An Exploratory Study of the Assaultive Experience and Assaultive Potential of California Youth Authority Wards." *Journal of Research in Crime and Delinquency* 9: 171–96.

Weston, Paul B., and Kenneth M. Wells. 1974. *Criminal Investigation: Basic Perspectives.* Second Edition. Englewood Cliffs, N. J.: Prentice-Hall.

Weyhrich, Joseph H. 1968. "Representing the Juvenile in the Adjudicatory Hearing." *St. Louis University Law Journal* 12: 466–93.

White, Stephen. 1971. "The Presentation in Court of Social Inquiry Reports." *Criminal Law Review* 1971: 629–37.

"Youthful Offenders and Adult Courts: Prosecutorial Discretion vs. Juvenile Rights." 1973. *University of Pennsylvania Law Review* 121: 1184–93.

Zakouro, James P. 1972. "Trial by Jury in Adjudicational Stage of State Juvenile Court Delinquency Proceedings Not Constitutionally Required." *University of Kansas Law Review* 20: 369–76.

Zekas, Joseph P. 1973. "Constitutional Law: Juvenile Waiver Statute: Delegation of Legislative Power to Judiciary." *Wisconsin Law Review* 1973: 259–68.

INDEX